COCKTAIL TECHNIQUES

COCKTAIL TECHNIQUES

Kazuo Uyeda

MUD PUDDLE BOOKS

NEW YORK

Cocktail Techniques
by Kazuo Uyeda

Copyright © 2000 by Kazuo Uyeda
Original Japanese edition published by SHIBATA SHOTEN Co., Ltd.

English language translation by Marc Adler/Trustforte Language Services

Phillip Hanson provided invaluable assistance in the preparation of this
English language edition.

English language translation
Copyright © 2010 by Mud Puddle Books, Inc.

This English language edition is published by arrangement with SHIBATA
SHOTEN Co., Ltd., Tokyo, through the Tuttle-Mori Agency, Inc., Tokyo

Mud Puddle Books, Inc.
54 W. 21st Street
Suite 601
New York, NY 10010
info@mudpuddlebooks.com

ISBN: 978-1-60311-214-7

All rights reserved. No part of this book may be reproduced or transmitted in any
form or by any means, electronic or mechanical, including photocopying, recording,
or by any information storage and retrieval system, without permission in writing
from the publisher.

Printed in China

CONTENTS

FOREWORD TO THE ORIGINAL EDITION 11

BASICS 13
Welcome to the World of Cocktails 13

MAKING GOOD COCKTAILS 15
The Language of Cocktails 15
Boosting Your Focus 16
Reading Taste Buds 17
The Way of the Cocktail 18

SHAKING TECHNIQUE 22
The Hard Shake—Overview 22
First Encounter 22
Perfecting the Hard Shake 24
Suitable Ingredients 24
Fine Shards of Ice 26

STIRRING TECHNIQUE 31
Overview 31
Stirring and Ice 31
The Ideal Stir 31

BUILDING TECHNIQUES 38
Three Types of Builds 38
    With Carbonated Ingredients 38
    Without Carbonated Ingredients 38
    Pousse-Café Style 39
Good to the Last Drop 39

BASIC TECHNIQUES 43
Every Movement Counts 43
How the Pros Do It 43
    Holding the Bottle 44
    Removing the Cap 45

Measuring Out Ingredients	46
Cracking Ice	47
Peeling Lemons	50
Holding the Glass	51
Polishing the Glass	52
Layering	52
Rim Frosting	53
Coral Frosting	54
Cutting Fruit	55

WHITE SPIRITS ... 57
The Light Appeal of White Spirits ... 57
White Spirits Suited to a Hard Shake ... 57
- Gin ... 57
- Vodka ... 58
- Rum ... 58
- Tequila ... 59

BROWN SPIRITS ... 60
Heart and Soul-Brown Spirits ... 60
Scotch Whiskey's Unique Flavor ... 60
The Charm of Bourbon ... 61
Grape Brandy and Apple Brandy ... 62
How to Drink Dark Rum ... 62

LIQUEURS ... 64
The Charm of Liqueurs ... 64
What Liqueurs Are and How They Are Made ... 64
Characteristics of Liqueurs ... 65
Selecting Liqueurs ... 65

TOOLS ... 67
Shaker vs. Mixing Glass ... 67
Types and Uses of Shakers ... 67
Choosing a Shaker ... 67
Choosing a Mixing Glass ... 68

COCKTAIL GLASSES ... 70
An Essential Element for a Good Cocktail ... 70

STANDARD COCKTAILS ... 72
Gin-Base ... 73
- Martini ... 73
- Gibson ... 76
- Gimlet ... 78
- Alaska ... 80
- Gin & Bitters ... 82
- Gin & Tonic ... 84
- White Lady ... 86
- Gimlet Highball ... 88

Brandy-Base ... 90
- Sidecar ... 90
- Stinger ... 92
- Alexander ... 94
- Jack Rose ... 96
- Brandy Sour ... 98

Whiskey-Base ... 100
- Manhattan ... 100
- New York ... 102
- Old-Fashioned ... 104

Vodka-Base ... 106
- Russian ... 106
- Salty Dog ... 108
- Moscow Mule ... 110
- Sea Breeze ... 112

Rum-Base ... 114
- Daiquiri ... 114
- Bacardi ... 116
- Frozen Daiquiri ... 118

Tequila-Base ... 120
- Margarita ... 120

Liqueur-Base	122
Grasshopper	122
Valencia	124
Charlie Chaplin	126
Wine-Base	128
Bellini	128
Bamboo	130
Kir Royal	132
Categories of Shaken Cocktails	134
Original Cocktails	135
How Colors Add to Flavor	135
Prize Winners	138
Pure Love ~ My First Prize Winner	138
Fantastic Léman	140
Tokio	142
City Coral	146
King's Valley	148
Jealousy	150
Left Alone	152
Japanese Seasons	154
Shungyo	154
Sumidagawa Boshoku	156
Hideriboshi	158
Sekishu	160
Yukitsubaki	162
Coral Frosted-Style Cocktails	164
Cosmic Coral	164
Castary Coral	166
Crystal Coral	168
Coral 21	170
Miscellaneous	172
M-30 Rain	172
Blue Trip	174

Hong Kong Connection	176
Fishermen & Son	178
$K\alpha\lambda o\varsigma\ K\nu\mu\alpha$	180
Miracle	182
Maria Elena	184
Lahaina 45	186
Moon River	188
Southern Whisper	190
M-45 Subaru	192
Fraise Richesse	194
Brume d'Or	196
Tender Series	198
T-1 Tender One	200
T-2 Tender Two	200
Index	201
About the Author	208

INTRODUCTION

FOREWORD TO THE ORIGINAL EDITION

The golden age of cocktails in Japan stretched for more than two decades from their initial popularity at end of World War II until around 1968. The cocktail boom peaked in 1964, the year of the Tokyo Olympics. At that time you could find a Martini shaker in every house and a Martini glass in every hand.

Cocktails entered Japan together with other western alcoholic drinks and spread rapidly, riding the postwar wave of Western culture. If you were an adult member of society, you were expected to know how to drink a cocktail. The art of making cocktails was described by some as an "instantaneous art" that required the refinement of all six senses. Cocktails represented a bottomless well of dreams and romance.

It didn't take very long after cocktails took off in Japan for a unique Japanese style to take shape, a style that was influenced not only by the Japanese national character but also the country's temperament and even the climate. Flavors were isolated, techniques were polished and, in the end, an unmistakably Japanese style of mixing was born.

At one time people would go outside Japan in search of good cocktails, but today I repeatedly hear stories of people who return from such trips disappointed. I think simple differences are a factor in this. One difference is that Japanese culinary preferences favor subtle shadings over the impact of one strong flavor. Another difference is the Japanese attention to detail. Indeed, a major factor is the growing quality of Japanese bartenders, who devote a great deal of energy to honing their skills and who know that maximum effort translates into a richer experience for the guest.

I personally believe the best cocktails in the world are to be found today in Japan ~ just look at the number of Japanese bartenders taking prizes in cocktail-mixing contests throughout the world.

When the offer to write a technical book on making cocktails came to me at my bar, I was more than aware that I myself am still in the process of learning the craft. What you hold in your hands is the sum of my knowledge and techniques accumulated over the years. These may not be for everyone, but it's also a fact that many of the techniques I have developed and which have gained general acceptance, (such as the hard shake, the three-point shake and the Tokyo Kaikan stir, to name a few) have been followed incorrectly and often with disappointing results. One of my motivations in writing this book was to communicate the importance of the philosophy behind cocktail mixing, as well as to describe techniques like the hard shake more accurately.

Bartending is a service industry. As such, bartenders are required to have the ability to interact with guests honestly and forthrightly, and it is important for that honesty and forthrightness to shape the mixing of every drink. And while achieving the desired flavor is obviously the ultimate goal, there are many paths that lead to that summit, which means that approaching the art of mixing cocktails from many angles is an important part of mastering this art.

Cocktails encompass a two-fold enjoyment: the enjoyment of drinking and the enjoyment of mixing. As bartenders, the mixing side of this equation is part of our job, and finding pleasure in it is very important. If a bartender doesn't enjoy mixing a cocktail, the guest won't enjoy drinking it. Therefore, the first thing you must do as a bartender is to learn how to enjoy mixing cocktails. After that, humility and hard work will be the foundation on which your skills will grow, never forgetting that the perfection of a cocktail must remain a healthy pursuit.

I hope this book serves as a valuable stepping-stone as you begin your journey.

—Kazuo Uyeda
July 2000

BASICS

WELCOME TO THE WORLD OF COCKTAILS

A cocktail is any drink made by mixing two or more ingredients, which means that even mixed juice drinks merit the name. However, for the purposes of this book we'll mainly be looking at drinks mixed with alcoholic ingredients.

Cocktails have been around since beer and wine were first drunk, although at that time they mostly consisted of mixing said beer or wine with hot or cold water. Cocktails first took their current form around 120 years ago after a German engineer named Carl von Linde invented a high-pressure cooling apparatus, thanks to which ice became widely available. The Gin Fizz, invented by the New Orleans bartender Henry C. Ramos in 1888, is famous for being the first cocktail to use ice. There are an almost infinite number of cocktail recipes today, but in the long history of alcoholic beverages this novel drink was unprecedented.

The fashion for dry drinks is as strong as ever today, even in cocktails. Martinis are a case in point – the stronger the preference for dryness, the lower the proportion of vermouth. You hear crazy stories of people who *add* vermouth by simply looking at a bottle of it while sipping straight gin. And there are all sorts of recipes that leave you scratching your head if you know what cocktails are supposed to be all about.

My Martinis, by the way, are not very dry. The Martini is actually based on a cocktail called a Gin & It, which is made by mixing equal amounts of a dry gin and an Italian sweet vermouth (*It* being short for *Italian*), so to think that gin alone could constitute a Martini is an obvious error. The whole point of the drink is the combination of the vermouth and the gin. What makes a cocktail a cocktail, after all, is the addition of other ingredients to a base ingredient in order to enhance or bring out the flavor of the base.

There are a few basic recipes that are considered standards, but no two cocktails will ever be identical. Different people mix drinks under different circumstances, and this variety is one of the delights of drinking cocktails. Show me a hundred different bartenders, and I'll show you a hundred different Martinis.

In this book I describe how I make cocktails. The techniques I use may not be for everyone, but what I can say is that they are the fruit of thirty-five years of dedication to this art.

MAKING GOOD COCKTAILS

THE LANGUAGE OF COCKTAILS

The technical skills needed for mixing cocktails require a certain type of emotional engagement from the bartender, and in order to achieve this engagement, you have to have a kind of dialogue with the recipes.

For example, let's assume you're going to make a Sidecar. Obviously, you want to make it so that it tastes good, but you also want to think about how the cocktail itself wants to be made. You have to look at the standard recipe (2:1:1) with this in mind. Every cocktail was invented by someone, so you have to imagine what it was that the creator wanted to achieve ~ what he wanted, what he was looking for ~ by creating this cocktail. Find out where and when the cocktail was created, and think about how much of your own personality you can blend into that. You use the standard recipe as a framework within which you create your own unique cocktail. This process is vital.

Bartenders are often praised for particular drinks. One bartender makes fantastic Martinis. Another makes Sidecars that are out of this world. They have succeeded because they dug deeper into the cocktail and created something uniquely their own. You'll never make a unique cocktail by sticking exactly to the recipe. You have to engage the cocktail, ask it what it needs to make it better. As you work through this process, you'll begin adding your own original touches. It's an unconscious process, which means that even when you make the same 2:1:1 cocktail, there will always be a difference in the resulting taste.

That said, you couldn't skip the process of learning the basic technique of making that 2:1:1 Sidecar. Without that foundation, you won't be able to make anything. It's only after mastering that foundation that you can start to focus on improving the flavor. The emotional engagement I talked about above is built on this foundation of basic technique.

BOOSTING YOUR FOCUS

When I talk about *focus* I often use the phrase *apply your mind*. "You're not applying your mind to your work" or "your work lacks focus" are the kinds of things you might hear from a boss. The same is true of focusing in sports, for example. Focusing the powers of your mind is an important ability.

Of all the different cocktail techniques out there, I often hear people complain that they don't know how to make stirred cocktails taste better. My belief is that it depends on whether you're applying your mind to it. The resulting flavor of a drink hinges on the degree to which you apply yourself to making a good cocktail and how intensely you can focus your mind on that one goal. Someone who lacks that feeling won't make a good cocktail, no matter how *perfectly* he or she mixes it. Therefore, your ability to nurture this kind of focus is an important factor in making good cocktails.

So what does it mean to apply your mind? Well, it varies from person to person, but there is something universal in the way that you put your heart into making a cocktail for a guest you like (or for someone you love). Something special happens in that situation, and the result is special, too. Why does this happen? It happens because there was something different about your state of mind. This is what you have to recreate, but you have to experience it at least once in order to recreate that state of mind. So the questions are: what situations allow you to achieve that feeling, and can you take the opportunity when it presents itself? If you don't let that opportunity pass you by, then you'll make a good cocktail; and once you've done that, all you have to do is recreate that feeling.

I'm sure you've had the experience of finding yourself focusing your mind very intently in an unconscious way on a particular job. Being able to recognize the difference between a good cocktail and a very good cocktail is the same as the ability to be aware that you are intently focusing your mind. If you can feel energy running up and down your spine, and you can repeat the experience, then you'll be able to boost your ability to apply your mind to your work.

Unfortunately, if you can't feel that you are applying yourself, then you won't be able to maintain that image. You'll have lots of opportunities to feel this in the course of your career, but only as long as you stay open and aware. You have to make an effort to maintain an awareness of that feeling. Your success will depend on how far you can take that.

When I'm mixing cocktails behind the counter, I always stay aware of who's drinking what. Mixing a cocktail without knowing who's going to drink it is the epitome of not applying your mind. You can only apply your mind to your work if you know who's going to drink the cocktail you're making. Being aware of the purpose of what you're doing—and also *feeling* that purpose ~ will translate into improved cocktail-mixing skills.

The first step is to make an effort to feel this when making one or two of the, say, fifty cocktails you make in one day. You can mix a million cocktails over the course of your life, but if you don't apply your mind in this way, you'll never improve. This is fundamental for nurturing your focus.

READING TASTE BUDS

What I mean by *taste buds* is a guest's likes and dislikes. Knowing your guest's preferences is essential to making a good cocktail. In the service industry, you often hear the phrase "the guest's happiness is your happiness." This is true even if you're not on the frontlines dealing directly with guests, and it's an extremely important element in making cocktails. No matter how great a cocktail you make is, if the guest doesn't like it, then there's no point.

If a guest says she prefers cocktails with a bit of a kick, then make it that way for her. If another guest says he likes his cocktails on the sweet side, then you're not going to make him happy by making one that's dry. The ability to fine-tune each cocktail to the way each guest likes it is, after all, one of the great things about cocktails.

There was a famous bartender named Kiyoshi Imai (now passed

away) who, in his day, was known as Mr. Martini, and he used to say that for each cocktail, there are four recipes. The first is the standard recipe. The second is a recipe that has been modified to match current tastes. The third is the maker's own personal recipe. The fourth is the recipe that the guest likes. The ability to fine-tune cocktails in this manner is the essence of mixing cocktails, and a great bartender is someone who can fine-tune a cocktail to a guest's liking.

A male guest once ordered a City Coral at my bar, but I knew that no matter how I fine-tuned the City Coral, it would never match his preferences. So I suggested another cocktail for him. There's no cocktail in the world so great that absolutely everyone will like it. Success in our business depends almost entirely on the satisfaction of the guest, which means that an important part of our job is to know the guest's likes and dislikes and to select a cocktail that matches those preferences.

Once you've mastered the basic recipes for standard cocktails and succeeded in adding a bit of your own flair to them, then it's time to recognize that inside you there are cocktails both unique and original to you. In recent years there has been no dearth of contest winners who are young, studious and dedicated. This is a great thing, but in a way I feel bad for them. Before they've even mastered the standard cocktails, they're winning awards, which I feel has the effect of propelling them down the wrong path over the course of their rest of their careers.

Original cocktails are only worth anything if they are created on a solid foundation. Even people who have had success in contests can benefit from mastering the basic standards and then, on the basis of that, establishing their own cocktails.

THE WAY OF THE COCKTAIL

I often suspect that there is a *way of the cocktail* that defines how Japanese bartenders mix cocktails. In Japan we live surrounded by ancient rites and customs, each of which has its own particular rituals—*kado* (the way of the flower), *sado* (the way of tea), *judo* (the way of flexibility), *kendo* (the way of the sword), and so on. If you apply yourself with a similar degree of dedication to the art of making cocktails, there will be a *way of the cocktail* as well.

The kinds of cocktails Japanese bartenders make have undergone a unique transformation. This is possibly due to certain national traits such as the dedication to a particular path, a diligence and a knack for organization. Over the 75 year span since the cocktail came to Japan, a uniquely Japanese style has grown up around this American invention. It might not be too off the mark to say that the drinks mixed in Japan today are very true to the original spirit of each cocktail, and that the Japanese have stubbornly preserved the original form while pursuing ever greater heights in taste.

Westerners focus on results. While the Japanese have been influenced by this focus to a certain extent in recent years, we, at heart, respect the process. This quintessential national trait remains strong, as does a habit of praising sincerity of effort, irrespective of results. The same can be said about mixing cocktails. We have a certain sensibility whereby we tend to look closely at the way a cocktail is made and the effort that went into achieving a good taste. We focus not only on the flavor of the resulting cocktail but also on the process of mixing, and I believe that the effort put into mixing the cocktail contributes to its ultimate flavor.

Enjoying a cocktail is an experience that engages all of the guest's sense at once. The *taste* that is perceived through the eyes, the ears and the nose must be brought out. Human beings make final judgments about flavor in their brain, but before making that judgment many variables come into play. Which data is inputted into the brain before a cocktail is consumed is an important element in judging the flavor.

Experts say that the sensors on the human tongue are not absolute. When you eat something that you think will be good, your judgment generally coincides with your expectations. The same applies to cocktails. If you order a cocktail thinking that it's going to be good, it *will* be when you actually drink it. On the other hand if you think that it won't be good, the taste will be adversely affected. This is why Japanese bartenders focus so much on the process of mixing cocktails. Making guests feel that what they are about to drink is going to be delicious is key to creating the final flavor.

A guest opens a door, enters a bar, sits down and orders a drink. Everything that happens from that point until the cocktail is placed in front of her affects the flavor. If this particular guest has heard that "they make great cocktails at that bar," then she will probably be predisposed to think that any cocktail you serve her will be good.

In other words, the flavor of the cocktail is a result not only of the actions taken by the bartender in mixing the cocktail, but also of the way the human brain works. For example, guests tend to be extremely aware of the cleanliness of bartenders and of their personalities. So, the clothes you wear, your manner of speaking, how you look at people, your focus, your hygiene—all of these things go into creating flavor. If, for whatever reason, a guest decides that he doesn't want a particular bartender to mix his drinks, then any cocktail that bartender serves him will, without a doubt, taste subpar, and the guest will probably never visit that bar again.

The effort that guests see you putting into making cocktails is part of what creates the flavor. As I've said, the ultimate arbiter of the flavor of the cocktail that you make is the guest. No matter how much effort you put into making a cocktail, if the guest says the cocktail is no good, then that's that. You have to keep in mind that there are no absolutes when it comes to the flavor of the cocktails you make.

Stubborn ramen chefs or *stubborn* sushi chefs are staples of Japanese TV. According to the stereotype, the chef decides what's good and if a guest doesn't like it, he can go to hell. That may have some kind of entertainment value, but in the real world, things work differently. It's important to have the self-confidence to know your own tastes, but overconfidence can be dangerous. This is probably the most important aspect of the way of the cocktail. Never be arrogant. You might win every contest. Good for you, but that may mean nothing to a guest.

Your most important job as a bartender is to think about how you can make a cocktail that the guest will think is great. Never forget this. This is fundamental if you want to master the way of the cocktail.

Sumo wrestlers have a word that is very fitting in this situation, *shingitai*, which means *heart, technique and physique*. For a bartender this means a heart that is not overconfident or arrogant, the technical ability to realize the desire to make the best cocktail you can, and a physique that makes this possible (i.e., a healthy body).

It is often said that cocktail mixing is a line of work defined by brief encounters. Partly this means that each cocktail you make is different, but it also means that you'll only ever meet most of your guests once. You must work to value these encounters by keeping your bar open as often as possible. Further, sickness prevents you from applying your mind. Therefore, remember: don't drink too much and stay in control of your health.

I've talked about a lot of different things here, but the most important thing as you travel along the way the cocktail is to stay healthy and do your best.

SHAKING TECHNIQUE

THE HARD SHAKE—OVERVIEW

Shaking is a technique used for chilling and mixing ingredients in a cocktail shaker with ice. Shaking is particularly suited to mixing ingredients that have different densities (i.e., specific gravities) or that are otherwise difficult to mix, such as mixing relatively light spirits together with denser liqueurs, creams, egg whites, fruit juices and so on.

Every bartender has a unique shaking method, but all share one common goal: to chill and mix as well as to take the edge off the flavor of the ingredients and the alcohol; in other words, to make a smoother cocktail. I developed the hard shake in order to achieve this goal.

As the name implies, a hard shake means shaking the shaker hard in an intricate pattern. At the opposite end of the spectrum is a soft shake. A skilled bartender can use either method to mix ingredients. So why do I choose a hard shake?

Let me describe what I picture a shake should be. Imagine the constituent element of alcohol as a square. Most people tend to think of shaking as a way of rounding the sharp corners of that square, but as I see it, I'm forcing air into that square causing it to puff out and become rounder. In other words, the aeration acts like a cushion that prevents the bite of the ingredients and the sharpness of the alcohol from directly attacking the tongue. The bubbles expand the alcohol, and the flavor becomes softer. Those constituent elements of the alcohol which are bunched together gradually become one. This is the way I visualize what's happening when I shake the shaker.

Creating aeration is the ultimate goal of my hard shake.

FIRST ENCOUNTER

It's strange, but even if a cocktail is made exactly according to the recipe, the final product will differ in flavor and color from bartender to bartender. It was after I first noticed this that my method of mixing cocktails began to change.

My desire to make the best possible cocktail for my guests required me to focus my energy on shaking the shaker, and after a while I noticed that very small bubbles would form inside my cocktails. Guests would tell me that the sharpness of the alcohol was softened in my cocktails, and it was then that I understood the importance of the bubbles. Creating these small, soft bubbles inside my cocktails became a very important task.

In search of a better cocktail I also began to change the way I shook the shaker. At first, I used a broader angle when I shook the shaker, but this didn't create enough bubbles. So I introduced a more forceful three-point shake in order to thoroughly mix the ingredients. To create a more complex motion, I introduced a snap and then a twist while I held the shaker diagonally. And that's how the hard shake was born.

Shakers come in different sizes: one serving (small), two servings (medium), three servings (large) and five servings (extra large). Professionals use the medium size and up. When I make a cocktail for one or two people, I use a large shaker. Unlike mixing glasses, the large shaker can act as a small shaker.

Parts of the shaker. From left: body, strainer, top.

This method added another level of complexity to the creation of the flavor of the cocktail. Over the next five years after this discovery, I made hundreds of cocktails, perfecting an efficient hard shake and eliminating the need for excessive motion. The actual shaking motion became more compact and, at the same time, more complex and intricate. Also, my method was influenced by the realization that exaggerated motion reduced the intricacy of the shaking.

My current style was established over twenty years ago. Just because it goes by a single name, however, doesn't mean that I do it the same every time. I vary the strength and the length of time of the shaking according to the ingredients I'm using. I also add a twist and a snap to create an intricate motion.

PERFECTING THE HARD SHAKE

Because ice is used in shaking, chilling the ingredients is not a problem. The real challenge is in mixing the ingredients. The ability to achieve a thorough mixing is the whole point of the hard shake. Performing a hard shake vigorously and for a long time without the necessary mixing skills will only result in the ice melting inside the shaker, which will make the cocktail watery. If the mixing is done correctly, however, the water from the melted ice can be drawn into the alcohol without watering down the flavor.

The only way to tell whether you have mastered the hard shake or not is by tasting the result, and the only criterion of judgment is whether it is watery or not. If the ingredients have not been properly mixed, the result tastes loose and unfocused. That said, you could judge a cocktail that uses cream or egg white visually. A skillful hard shake of these cocktails will result in a smooth whipped state. Therefore, these drinks are ideal for practicing the hard shake.

SUITABLE INGREDIENTS

There are a few ideal ingredients for bringing out the best of the hard shake. First and foremost are creams. If a cream is shaken correctly, it's agitated in a way that produces bubbles that result in a whipped state. This whipped state can be easily maintained if some kind of sweetener is added, and therefore, a consistency impossible with other shaking methods can be achieved.

Another ingredient that benefits from a hard shake is fruit juice. The way the bubbles are formed is no different than with other ingredients, but fruit juices are particularly hard to mix. The hard shake is especially suited to thoroughly mixing fruit juices with other ingredients because it reduces the acidity of the fruit juice and combines the juice with the alcohol to bring all the ingredients together into a single, consistent flavor.

Therefore, cocktails that are mixed by combining cream, egg white or fruit juice with a base liquor are particularly suited to the hard shake.

This shaking style doesn't bring out the best in certain combinations, for example, cocktails that are only combinations of liqueurs, spirits and other alcoholic ingredients. Bubbles can be created in these drinks, but they are difficult to maintain and disappear very quickly. Therefore, for the purposes of this book, I suggest stirring three cocktails that are ordinarily shaken ~ the Stinger, the Alaska and the Russian ~ because I think that stirring is capable of achieving an excellent flavor for these cocktails.

Moreover, some brands of liquor are more suitable as a base than others. The hard shake works by bringing separate ingredients in a shaker together into a unified whole. If the character and presence of the alcohol are lost in the final product, then the drink is no good, so you have to select a brand that has the necessary strength of character to survive the hard shake.

Variations in flavor are particularly notable among various brands of gin and vodka. Vodka is a drink that has the simple flavor of alcohol, but, strangely enough, you can see a very large difference when it's used in a cocktail. In general, the more delicious a liquor is when drunk by itself (e.g., if it has a very refined flavor), the less suited it is to the hard shake. Brands that maintain the bite of the alcohol when mixed into a cocktail are the ones that you will want to look to use in a hard shake.

FINE SHARDS OF ICE

The fine shards of ice that cover the surface of the cocktail are a side effect of the hard shake and not the ultimate goal. When I was developing the hard shake I spent a lot of time trying to create this layer of ice shards, even going so far as enlarging the holes in the strainer, but I now realize that that was a mistake. The most important thing in the hard shake is creating the bubbles.

If you perform the hard shake correctly, you will get these fine shards of ice without making the holes in the strainer bigger. Not only that, but if the ice spins inside the shaker, then a thin layer of ice will float on the surface. If you perform a hard shake by moving the shaker in a straight line in order to make the ice hit the bottom of the shaker, the ice will break into large pieces that won't be able to pass through the strainer. Even if the ice does, all you will get is little chunks of ice and not fine shards.

TECHNIQUE

1. Completely fill the shaker with ice, smaller pieces on the bottom and larger pieces on the top, using equal amounts of cracked ice and ice cubes.

2. Fill the shaker with water to get rid of corners and small pieces of ice (one cause of watery cocktails) and also to chill the shaker. Holding the ice in with your hand, tip the shaker upside down and pour out the water.

3. Pour the ingredients into the shaker, working from largest to smallest amount.

4. Place the strainer portion of the shaker on the body making sure it is level. If it is loose or crooked, it can come off during shaking.

5. Pause for the length of a breath to let the air out of the shaker, and then put the top on. If the air is not allowed to exit, the top could pop off during shaking.

6. Shake. Mix the ingredients making efficient use of the interior of the shaker. Cocktails using cream, egg whites, egg yolk or other hard-to-mix ingredients should be shaken 50% longer than normal.

7. Pour into a chilled cocktail glass.

SHAKING TECHNIQUE

I. HOLDING THE SHAKER

1. Hold your left hand in front of your chest. Place the shaker in your hand with the top towards you. Press on the bottom of the shaker with the middle and ring fingers of your left hand.

2. Curve the palm of your hand to prevent it from pressing against the body of the shaker.

3. Press down on the top with the thumb of your right hand.

4. Place the index finger of your right hand on the shoulder of the strainer.

5. Grip the body with your middle finger and the strainer with your index finger.

6. Place your other fingers gently on the body. The photograph shows how you want to hold the shaker.

TYPES OF ICE

Cracked ice and ice cubes are used in a 6:4 ratio. The shake becomes stiff if only cracked ice is used, so ice cubes are used as a cushion. Using ice cubes is also less expensive.

SHAKING TECHNIQUE

2. STANCE

Stand naturally with your feet apart, approximately at shoulder width. From this stance place your left foot out at a 45° angle, and hold the shaker above your left foot, turning your upper body 45° to the left.

SHAKE

A single shake comprises two motions: throwing the shaker out and bringing it back in. The ice bounces against the bottom of the shaker and then against the strainer. It's important to bring the shaker back faster than the ice bouncing off the bottom of the shaker. Accordingly, you should hear the ice bouncing twice during a single shake.

Once you have mastered this, the sound of each bounce should be the same. You're not doing it right if you hear the ice rattling around during the length of the shake, or if the ice hitting the bottom of the shaker is louder than when it hits the strainer.

1. Using the correct grip, hold the shaker in front of your left breast and quickly push it straight forward.

2. Return it to the original position. It is important that the ice hit the back of the shaker cleanly; try to create a sharp cracking sound.

SNAP

During this basic motion of throwing the shaker out and pulling it back in, add a snap with your wrist, changing the vertical angle of the shaker.

1. Snap your wrist when throwing the shaker out so that the shaker becomes upright.

2. When pulling the shaker back, snap your wrist again, this time putting the shaker upside down.

TWISTING: CHANGING THE HORIZONTAL ANGLE

Add a twist by raising your right shoulder and right elbow up. When throwing the shaker out twist it to the left. By shaking, snapping and twisting the shaker in this way, you can achieve a shake that makes the ingredients flow against each other inside the shaker. The following photographs show only the twist and the angle.

SHAKING TECHNIQUE

1. By raising your right shoulder and elbow while shaking, you can apply a screw-like twisting motion to the shaker. You can see that the shaker is being twisted just by looking at the motion of your left wrist. Remember that the shaker is not shaken straight forward and back, but with the angle as shown in photo (A). The barspoon shown in the photograph points straight away from the body. The shaker should be shaken at an angle to the barspoon.

2. Pull the shaker back towards the left part of your chest while twisting it.

3. POURING

The shaker is ordinarily held at an angle when pouring, but I pour vertically so that the fine shards of ice cover the entire surface of the cocktail glass.

1. Pour the contents of the shaker straight down moving the shaker counterclockwise.

2. After the contents are out, hold the shaker horizontally and snap it up and down to make the ice rattle inside. This final flourish has the effect of showing that your work is done, and that nothing is left inside the shaker.

Note: If you are uncertain about your measurements you may be prone to holding the shaker like this while pouring. However, if held this way, the shards of ice will be trapped in the curve of the shaker's shoulder.

SHAKING TECHNIQUE

STIRRING TECHNIQUE

OVERVIEW

Together with shaking, stirring is a pillar of cocktail mixing technique. Stirring is used for chilling and mixing ingredients that are relatively easy to mix such as ingredients with similar densities or when mixing cocktails that only use spirits.

It is often said that shaking takes the bite off the alcohol and stirring leaves it in, and this is true. You should stir cocktails when you want to emphasize the power and intensity of the base liquor. But stirring doesn't simply leave the characteristics of the spirit as it is: it also adds a certain richness and depth of flavor.

STIRRING AND ICE

Like shaking, stirring heavily depends on the kind of ice that is used. To minimize the risk of watering down the resulting cocktail, you have to wash the ice and consider the balance of the different sizes. But the most important thing when stirring is to avoid damaging the ice. Pieces of ice bump against each other when stirred, breaking off corners. When corners of the ice break off, they melt and water down the ingredients. The actual method of mixing is paramount in order to achieve the correct blending of the ingredients with some water from the ice without causing the ice to melt. The number of stirs and the speed of the stirring are adjusted to match the ingredients (liquors) being used and the state of the ice. Who is doing the stirring also affects the result. Some people can achieve a perfect mixture with a few turns of the spoon whereas others can stir for minutes without achieving anything. It really depends on the experience of the bartender.

THE IDEAL STIR

When the ingredients are poured into the mixing glass, they are unmixed and just sit there side by side. If you shake them, they split up and expand with the creation of bubbles. The idea is to unite the two ingredients together quietly. It's like weaving silk.

What you want to do is quietly but rapidly fuse together the molecules of liquor that are floating side by side in the glass. Once you have washed the ice and started pouring the ingredients, you should begin to focus. Your focus should increase when you start stirring. Ease your concentration when you remove the barspoon from the mixing glass, pour the drink and put it down in front of the guest. Relax. You're done. This is my image of how stirring should be done.

Tools needed for stirring. From left: strainer, mixing glass, barspoon. Most barspoons are angled at the neck, but I bend them straight so that the thickness of the spoon handle and head is as thin as possible to minimize damage to the ice during stirring.

Stir. That's all it says in the recipe, but inside the mixing glass a mysterious fusion quietly occurs during the stirring process.

TEMPERATURE CHART

Cracked ice is purchased from a specialized dealer. Ice cubes are the cubes created in an ordinary freezer.

Condition		Temperature °C	Increase in Volume ml
Temperature changes and increase in volume by type of ice.			
Cracked ice	Large; 2 pieces; Room Temperature 20°C; 20 stirs; Volume. 60 ml	8.0	10
Cracked ice	Small; 10 pieces; Room temperature 20°C 20 stirs; Volume 60 ml	4.5	17
Cracked ice	Mixed small and large; 6 pieces; Room temperature 20°C; 20 stirs; Volume 60 ml	4.0	13
Ice cubes	8 pieces; Room temperature 20°C; 20 stirs Volume 60 ml	6.0	15
Temperature changes and increase in volume by temperature of gin and type of ice			
Room temperature gin	20°C; Ice cubes; 8 pieces; 20 stirs	6.0	15
Refrigerated gin	7°C; Ice cubes; 8 pieces; 20 stirs	3.8	10
Refrigerated gin	7°C; Cracked ice; 6 pieces; 20 stirs	3.2	9
Refrigerated gin	7°C; Cracked ice; 6 pieces; 30 stirs	1.9	10
Temperature changes and increase in volume by number of stirs			
10 stirs	Room temperature; °20C; Ice cubes 8 pieces	7.0	10
15 stirs	Room temperature; 20°C; Ice cubes 8 pieces	6.3	12
20 stirs	Room temperature; 20°C; Ice cubes 8 pieces	6.0	15
30 stirs	Room temperature; 20°C; Ice cubes 8 pieces	3.9	16

My experiments show that the following conditions are ideal:

1. Refrigerated gin (5-7°C)
2. 25-30 stirs
3. Mix large and small pieces of cracked ice
4. Moderately rapid stirring

Variations may have occurred due to the temperature of the room in which the experiments were carried out. A thermometer and a cylinder were used for measurement.

STIRRING TECHNIQUE

1. Place the appropriate amount of cracked ice into the mixing glass and pour water over the ice.

2. Lightly stir the ice with the barspoon to melt the surface of the ice and break small corners off as well as to chill the mixing glass.

3. Place the strainer on the glass.

4. Tilt the mixing glass diagonally at about 45° and pour out all the water.

5. Remove the strainer and pour the ingredients into the glass starting with the base liquor.

6. Insert the barspoon into the mixing glass, slide it down the inside of the glass and stir. Make certain that the ice doesn't collide or break inside the glass. Hold the mixing glass on the very bottom (where there is no liquid) with your left hand to avoid heating the glass.

STIRRING TECHNIQUE

7. Place the strainer on the glass and pour the ingredients into a chilled cocktail glass.

8. When the mixing glass is empty, tilt it back a little (see photograph) and shake it vertically to rattle the ice, indicating that you are finished.

1. AMOUNTS OF ICE

The following photographs show the required amounts of ice and liquor placed in the mixing glass. (A) Shows how the ice and liquor should look from the side, and (B) shows the same from above. (C) Is a bad example with too much ice.

It goes without saying that ice is used for chilling ingredients during stirring and must therefore come in contact with the ingredients. Any ice that does not come in contact with the ingredients is not only wasted but melts and mixes in with the ingredients making the drink watery. Unlike shaking, in which there can't be too much ice, there is a proper amount of ice to use when stirring.

STIRRING TECHNIQUE

2. HOLDING THE BARSPOON

I hold the center of the barspoon when stirring, because, by holding the barspoon in this way, the head spins around very gracefully. With the barspoon held horizontally, place your thumb and ring finger on top and your index finger and middle finger below. Support the weight of the barspoon with your thumb and index finger and create the stirring motion with your middle finger and ring finger.

3. USING A BARSPOON

The ice and ingredients placed in the mixing glass spin when stirred, but you should not use a circular motion with your hand. Rather, you should stir with a back-and-forth motion.

With the barspoon always pressed against the inside of the mixing glass to avoid breaking the ice, repeat the back-and-forth motion of photographs (2)-(3), thus causing the ice and ingredients inside the glass to gently spin. Do not stir too slowly.

1. Place the barspoon diagonally between the mixing glass and the ice with the back of the spoon against the inside of the mixing glass. It is important not to move the ice during insertion. Maintain this angle and the relative positions of the ice and the spoon during stirring.

2. Push the barspoon away from yourself with your ring finger. It is mainly the strength of your ring finger that is used for stirring.

STIRRING TECHNIQUE

3. Next, pull the spoon back towards yourself with your middle finger. If you yank it back, you will produce waves in the liquor.

4. HOLDING THE MIXING GLASS

1. Place the strainer on the mixing glass so the handle of the strainer is pointing away from the pouring lip of the glass. Press down on the strainer with your index finger.

2. Hold the mixing glass firmly between your thumb and middle finger.

3. *How not to do it.* Hold all your fingers against the mixing glass or press your palm firmly against it. Because your body heat will raise the temperature of the mixing glass, this method should be avoided.

BAD EXAMPLE

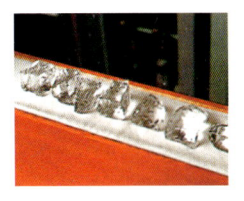

SIZES OF ICE

Use different sizes of cracked ice. If all the ice is small, it tends to melt quickly; if all the ice is large, then the total surface area of the ice drops, increasing the amount of time required to cool the ingredients. In short, ice should not all be of uniform size

STIRRING TECHNIQUE

BUILDING TECHNIQUES

THREE TYPES OF BUILDS

Building is a way of mixing a cocktail inside a glass without using any special tools. Think of a Whiskey & Soda, for example. You build the cocktail by pouring the different ingredients directly into a glass with ice. Broadly speaking, there are three types of builds.

1. With Carbonated Ingredients

This type uses a carbonated ingredient such as soda, tonic water or ginger ale. Examples include a Gin & Tonic and a Moscow Mule. Because the refreshing quality of the carbonation defines the flavor, you have to handle the ingredients carefully so that the carbonation isn't lost. Therefore, it's important not to overmix them. Overmixing the ingredients makes the drink flat and dulls the flavor.

Carbonated water should be poured directly onto the other ingredients in between the pieces of ice and not directly onto the ice. The carbonation will be lost if it directly hits a hard surface. Another thing to keep in mind is that, unlike ice in a shaken or stirred cocktail, the role of the ice in a built cocktail is only to keep the drink chilled. Accordingly, whether you use carbonation or not, the ingredients of the cocktail should be chilled ahead of time in the refrigerator. Otherwise, the ice will melt and water down the drink.

2. Without Carbonated Ingredients

Examples include a Rusty Nail and a Black Russian. If the ingredients do not mix well, you can give them some help with a little bit of stirring, but be careful not to overstir. When you add the ingredients, start with the lighter ones. As you add the heavier ones, they will naturally seep down into the lighter ingredients and mix by themselves.

The essence of a built cocktail is the natural mixing that occurs through pouring. This allows you to enjoy the flavors of the different ingredients separately. If the ingredients would taste better mixed completely, they should be stirred.

3. Pousse-Café Style

The term *pousse-café* literally means *pushes the coffee* in French and is used to mean a *coffee chaser* (an after-dinner drink or any other kind of digestif).

A typical pousse-café drink is an Angel's Kiss (or Angel's Tip), which is made by pouring ingredients having different specific gravities (densities) in layers into a liqueur glass or a small pousse-café glass. This could actually be called the *original build*. The ingredient with the highest specific gravity is poured first along the barspoon and down into the glass. Note that the same liquor can have different specific gravities depending on the brand. Also, remember that the indications in specific gravity charts tend to be approximations, so you have to determine the exact specific gravity for yourself.

GOOD TO THE LAST DROP

Building tends to be viewed as easier than shaking or stirring, but, in reality, a slightly different handling of the barspoon can totally change the flavor of the drink. This is particularly true of long drinks, which can take 15 to 20 minutes to consume. The skill level of the bartender becomes clearer with every sip.

For example, take a Gin & Tonic. Carefully mix one as described on the following page. Be careful not to lose the carbonation. Now make another one, but this time pour the tonic directly onto the ice and give it a few vigorous vertical thrusts with a spoon. For the first sip, the second one has a fresher, more invigorating taste since the bubbles have been stirred up. Wait 30 seconds, though, and the flavor becomes very flat compared to the first one. You can guess what happens after that: the acidity and bitterness of the ingredients come to the fore, and the end result is a totally different cocktail.

Another thing to keep in mind is that if you use gin that has been chilled in the freezer to the point that frost has built up on the bottle, you will find that the resulting cocktail is going to taste heavy and thick even if it's properly made. In other words, the light, refreshing flavor that is characteristic of a Gin & Tonic won't be achieved.

When building cocktails, there is no step for chilling the ingredients, so the base liquor should be chilled ahead of time. Keeping the bottles in the freezer dulls the bouquet and palette of the drink however, so I prefer the refrigerator.

CARBONATED INGREDIENTS (GIN & TONIC)

1. Chill the tumbler just enough for it to fog up (left glass). The glass on the right has not been chilled.

2. Depending on the size of the glass, use two to four pieces of cracked ice that are on the large side. Avoid piling the ice up above the rim of the glass, since this makes the cocktail hard to drink and is not visually appealing.

3. Squeeze in a lime. Use one hand to block the lime juice from squirting the guest.

4. Pour in the gin.

5. Top up with tonic water, making certain not to pour it directly onto the ice. If needed, move the ice apart with a barspoon. You're going to need a spoon for the next step, so have it ready in your right hand.

BUILDING TECHNIQUES

6. Slide the barspoon into the glass without bumping the ice. Do not stir unless you are including fruit juice or other types of liquors.

7. Pull the barspoon out in the same way.

Note: There's a drink called a Gin Rickey that's made with gin, lime and carbonated water. It uses a half-cut lime and is given to the guest with a muddler inside the glass. All the bartender does is pour in the gin and carbonated water without mixing. The guest uses the muddler to adjust the sourness of the drink to his/her taste.

NON-CARBONATED INGREDIENTS (RUSTY NAIL)

1. Chill a rocks glass just enough so that it fogs up.

2. Place two or three pieces of cracked ice that are on the large side in the glass (enough so that the ice doesn't float in the drink). Make certain that the ice is not piled higher than the rim of the glass.

3. Pour, starting with the lighter ingredients. In this case, the first ingredient to go in is the base whiskey. Cocktails that are made on the rocks are typically combinations of different liquors.

BUILDING TECHNIQUES

4. Pour in the heaviest liqueur (Drambuie). When the heavier ingredients are poured, they naturally mix down into the lighter ingredients below.

5. Insert the barspoon and stir lightly. Do not overstir.

6. Pull the spoon out without moving it against the current.

POUSSE-CAFÉ STYLE

1. Pour in the heaviest ingredient first. The glass and liqueurs need not be chilled.

2. Place the back of the spoon against the inside of the glass.

3. Pour slowly along the back of a spoon. Start with the heaviest liqueur and finish with the lightest.

BASIC TECHNIQUES

EVERY MOVEMENT COUNTS

You take the bottle down from the shelf. You twist off the cap. The liquid streams into the glass. Every action is natural and the result of focused concentration. The bartender never shows off and yet nothing is accidental.

Your job as a bartender is to make good cocktails, but it is also important to make them look delicious. To refine your skills, you have to closely study not only flavors but also all the movements that go into making a cocktail. You have to practice the basics and focus on making your movements flow while presenting a clean, neat image.

The intent isn't to look cool but rather to refine the entire cocktail drinking experience for the guest. Herein lies the biggest difference between an amateur making cocktails at home and a professional bartender standing in front of the bar doing his job while all eyes are on him.

HOW THE PROS DO IT

Let's take a look at how to use a jigger. Remember that professional bartenders typically do not use jiggers. They acquire a feel for the different measurements through practice.

The most popular jigger used in bars has a cup that measures an ounce on one end and 1½ ounces on the other. If you're going to be measuring smaller amounts such as ⅓ ounce or ⅔ ounce, though, you'll still have to rely on feel to estimate by eye the cup's fullness. Even if you're measuring a perfect ounce, the shot you filled to brimming will be different from the shot you poured just a little short. Ultimately, even using a jigger, measuring amounts is dependent on feel and not an exact science.

On the other hand, if you're making drinks for a number of people and you're measuring out, say, five ounces of an ingredient, then you'll have to measure out one ounce five times. If there's any mistake in how much you're measuring out, your mismeasurement is going to get multiplied five times over. So, in the long run, you will achieve greater accuracy if you practice getting a feel for how much you're pouring out based on the elapsed time a liquid, having a certain thickness, pours out in a stream.

You have to refine your own feel, and this doesn't apply only to measurements. Bartending is a professional's job. You'll only be able to achieve the subtle differences in taste that match guests' preferences once you've weaned yourself off the jigger.

HOLDING THE BOTTLE

Hold the bottom third of the bottle with your right hand so that the label is visible. There are three reasons for this:

1. In this position, you have free movement of your wrist.

2. This position combines visual appeal with stability. Gripping the upper part of the bottle looks awkward.

3. When the liquor pours out of the bottle, it can drip down and stain the label. By holding the label up or to the side you can keep it clean.

Hold the bottom third of the bottle with the label facing up when pouring to keep the label clean. You can also hold the bottle so that the label is to the side, facing the guest. Holding the label face up provides more stability, however.

By holding the bottle at the proper position you are afforded a greater freedom of movement in your wrist, and your movements will look graceful.

THREE THINGS NOT TO DO

1. Hold the bottle near the top. This not only looks clumsy, but you also risk your hands getting dirty, which detracts from the professional image of cleanliness you must maintain.

BASIC TECHNIQUES

2. Grip the bottle above the label, which restricts the movement of your wrist.

3. Hold the bottle with the label facing down, which will cause the label to get dirty if the contents of the bottle drip down onto it.

REMOVING THE CAP

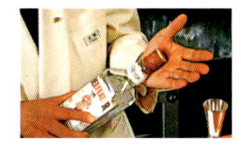

1. Grip the cap against your palm with the base of your thumb.

2. Hold the bottle with both hands turned inward. Holding the bottom third of the bottle makes this easier.

3. Turn both hands out simultaneously to remove the cap. A single turn should be sufficient to remove the cap. If not, the cap should come off with a second turn. Reverse this movement to close the bottle.

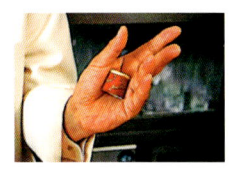

4. Grip the cap in the palm of your hand like this, leaving your fingers free to move. Putting the cap down halts the flow of motion and looks sloppy. Keep the cap in your hand until you close the bottle.

MEASURING OUT INGREDIENTS

1. ACQUIRING A FEEL

1. Begin by filling an empty bottle with water and practice pouring the liquid out in streams of a consistent thickness. You should be able to easily switch between two streams (thick and thin).

2. Practice using a jigger and pouring out the same amount using your two preferred stream thicknesses, getting a feel for the amount of time needed. Your goal should be to get comfortable pouring five different amounts: 1/3 ounce, 1/2 ounce, 2/3 ounce, 1 ounce and 1 1/2 ounce.

Practice by alternating between two different amounts, e.g., back and forth between 1 ounce and 1/2 ounce. If instead you repeat the same amount over and over, you will wind up trying to fine tune the previous pour, which defeats the purpose of practicing to acquire a feel that will allow you to pour a certain amount without adjustment. Your goal is to be able to pour out an exact amount the first time.

2. HOLDING THE JIGGER

The most popular type of jigger is a combination of 1 ounce and 1 1/2 ounce cups. When switching between the two, flip the cup using your index finger and your middle finger. Your thumb and index finger follow supporting the top and the bottom. Practice until you achieve a smooth motion.

1. Hold the jigger with your thumb, index finger and middle finger. This is done with the cap from the bottle still snug in the palm of your hand.

2. Flip the jigger over with your index finger and middle finger. Follow with your ring finger and hold the jigger with your index finger, middle finger and ring finger.

BASIC TECHNIQUES

3. USING A JIGGER

When measuring out a liquid it should flow from bottle to jigger to shaker in a smooth stream. (The jigger should actually be used only when pouring into a glass, of course.) Like a waterfall, the flow should never break. As soon as the jigger is full, its contents should be poured into the shaker.

Of course a professional bartender should practice pouring out amounts without using a jigger.

1. The bottle, the jigger and the shaker should form a straight line. Place the jigger right next to the shaker.

2. When the jigger is full, turn your wrist to pour the contents into the shaker.

CRACKING ICE

Just like wood, ice has a grain along which it can easily be cracked, so it's important to be able to find the grain. Always try to crack the ice along this grain. The only tool you need is an ice pick.

1. HOLDING THE ICE PICK

1. Hold the ice pick like this, using your palm as a stopper.

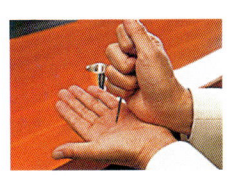

2. As shown in the photograph, grip the ice pick so that you don't jab your palm when the base of your right hand hits the palm of your left hand. You can injure yourself if you don't do this properly, so be extremely careful.

2. MAKING CRACKED ICE

Small pieces of ice are created by breaking a larger piece in half, then breaking those pieces in half, and so on—not by breaking smaller pieces off from the side of the large piece. The ice pick should hit the surface of the ice at a right angle.

1. Should you want to crack a large piece of ice down the middle across the grain, stabbing it forcefully with the ice pick will only cause it to crack along the grain. Instead, draw a straight line down the middle and tap it lightly in several locations along the line.

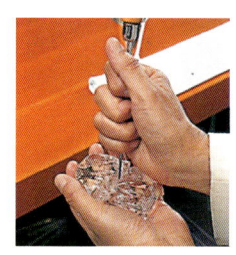

2. When this is done, crack it in the center.

3. The cracked ice. Keep cracking it down the middle, aiming for a rectangular shape.

4. Have the cracked ice along with ice cubes ready in an ice well.

BASIC TECHNIQUES

3. MAKING ICE SPHERES

This process involves chipping away at a block of ice with an ice pick to achieve an ice sphere that fits perfectly into a glass. Chipping off large chunks will not achieve this.

1. Get a large piece of ice.

2. Create a cube that is as long on one side as the diameter of the sphere that you want to create. The size can be approximate.

3. Once you have a cube, imagine a circle drawn on it.

4. Chip off the corners down along the circle.

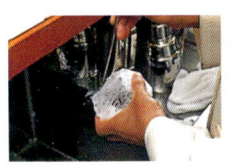

5. The idea is to create a cylinder shape with the circle's diameter.

6. The resulting cylinder of ice.

7. Now hold it lengthwise and chip away at the corners to create the sphere. Make the bottom a bit flatter so that it sits well in the bottom of a glass.

8. Round out the shape.

9. Put the sphere under the tap for a second to wash off bumps and small particles of ice, and then put it on a screen or similar surface that will allow excess water to run off. Leave it in the freezer overnight.

10. Remember: the surface easily melts, so do not wash it off before use.

PEELING LEMONS

Lemon peels contain two components: bitterness and aroma. The bitter component drips straight down, but the aroma component sprays out in a fine mist. It is this aroma mist that you want to use in a cocktail. This method is ideal when you want to add a bit of lemony zest to a cocktail.

1. Cut off a piece of lemon peel about the size of your thumb.

2. The center portion should be thicker than the edges with a bit of the white section left. This is to make sure that you can bend it easily.

BASIC TECHNIQUES

3. Hold the thin outer circumference between your thumb and middle finger.

4. With your index finger, press against the central portion and bend, creating a fine mist.

WHERE TO HOLD THE LEMON PEEL

Since the bitter component of the lemon drips straight down, you cannot hold the lemon peel directly above the glass. Instead, hold the lemon peel about 4 to 6 inches away from the rim of a glass at a 45° angle from the bottom of the glass. This allows the bitter component to drip straight down and miss the glass while the aroma component floats down and adds to the flavor of the cocktail.

HOLDING THE GLASS

Get into the habit of holding glasses by the bottom or the stem to prevent warming chilled cocktails with your body heat. Never hold a glass with your entire hand flat against it. It goes without saying that holding a glass by the rim is totally inexcusable.

POLISHING THE GLASS

After washing a glass with a neutral detergent, place it in hot water. Once the glass has warmed up, shake the water off and polish the glass while it is still wet. Use a long dishcloth (24 to 32 inches; a cotton/linen blend is preferable). It's preferable to divide the operation into two steps: 1) drying 2) polishing. Do not use a lot of force when polishing. Also, remember that using a dishcloth that has absorbed too much water can break the glass.

1. Drape the dishcloth over the thumb of your left hand.

2. Grip the bottom of the glass firmly with your left hand and push the dishcloth all the way into the glass.

3. Polish the inside of the glass with your thumb and the outside with your other fingers. Do not use too much force, and polish the inside and the outside the same time.

LAYERING

Layering is created by gently pouring a heavier ingredient into a lighter one, making the color darker at the bottom and lighter at the top. This is a way of creating an artistic display of colors for the guest, who then mixes the drink him or herself with a muddler to even out the flavor.

The example used here is a Singapore Sling, which uses cherry brandy. Another famous example is a Tequila Sunrise, which uses grenadine.

BASIC TECHNIQUES

Pour the cherry brandy slowly in a thin stream. A Singapore Sling is a gin-based long drink that is ordinarily shaken. The beautiful dark color of the cherry brandy stands out.

RIM FROSTING

Frosting the rim of a glass with a thin ring of sugar or salt not only appeals to the eyes but also adds flavor to the drink. Of course, it is important to use a uniform amount.

Some examples of frosted cocktails are a Salty Dog, a Margarita, a Kiss of Fire and a Yukiguni. The method is the same for whatever type of glass is used.

1. Put a thin layer of salt on a flat plate big enough around that the rim of the glass will fit inside. Have a half a lime cut and standing by. During the process, replace the salt occasionally, as it will crust due to the moisture from repeated use.

2. Place the rim of the glass at a 45° angle against the cross-section of the lime and give the glass one full turn to moisten the entire rim of the glass. Maintain this angle since it provides the most stability for the glass, resulting in a uniform area of the rim being moistened. This angle is also the easiest to establish visually.

3. Do not raise the glass as shown in the photograph, as the lime juice which has been applied to a uniform area around the rim of the glass will drip down, creating waves and making the ring of salt look sloppy around the rim.

4. Keeping the glass upside down, place the rim of the glass into the salt.

5. Tap the glass lightly with your finger to remove excess salt. Your frosted glass is now complete. You can replace the salt with sugar for a sugar frosting.

CORAL FROSTING

This style is a broader variation of the rim frosting and is intended to evoke a coral reef. Beside the City Coral, this method is used in the four original cocktails I created as part of the C&C Series that also includes the Cosmic Coral, the Castary Coral, and other cocktails all named starting with the letter C.

1. Place salt and blue curaçao in two shallow bowls. The salt should be as deep as the height of the coral effect you want to create, and the blue curaçao should be half of that height.

BASIC TECHNIQUES

2. Place the rim of the glass into the blue curaçao.

3. Without turning the glass right side up, push the glass straight into the salt.

4. Pull the glass straight out and remove the salt from inside. Your coral style glass is ready. You can create different coral style effects using melon liqueur or grenadine syrup.

CUTTING FRUIT

1. LEMONS AND LIMES

1. Cut off the top and bottom ends of the lemon/lime.

2. Cut down the middle, and then into three wedges.

3. Cut out the central white section.

4. Cut the ends off diagonally inward.

BASIC TECHNIQUES

5. One wedge of a lemon/lime cut into six equal wedges and trimmed (right).

6. Cut about two-thirds of the way down, leaving the yellow peel attached.

WHAT NOT TO DO

1. Do not make the peel portion too thick.

2. The reason for this is that when a guest tries to squeeze the lemon, the flesh will pop out like this, making it difficult to squeeze.

2. ORANGES

1. Cut an orange into four equal wedges and then into semicircles.

2. Make an incision about halfway into the semicircle and place on the rim of the glass.

3. Alternately, the incision can be diagonal into the fleshy part. Place on the rim of the glass.

BASIC TECHNIQUES

WHITE SPIRITS

THE LIGHT APPEAL OF WHITE SPIRITS

Alcoholic beverages are broadly divided into three types depending on how they are made: distilled beverages, fermented beverages and mixed alcohols (liqueurs).

A white spirit is a distilled alcohol that is colorless and transparent like vodka, gin, tequila and rum. These four liquors are commonly used bases in cocktails. Each is made using different ingredients and methods, and while they might look the same, they are totally dissimilar in smell and flavor. Each has its own unique character.

If you list the white spirits in order from the strongest character to the weakest, you have tequila, gin, rum and vodka. Vodka is supposed to have absolutely no character whatsoever. Each type of liquor has various subtypes and brands. Different brands of gin, for example, have different smells and taste and even have different proofs. This means that when you use one brand in a cocktail, you will have a different taste than if you had used a different brand. You should never leave the selection of ingredients to someone else, but rather choose the appropriate spirit after trying each one yourself.

Personally, I have different brands that I like for shaken cocktails, stirred cocktails, built cocktails, and when drinking straight. In this section I will mainly talk about white spirits that are particularly suited to shaken cocktails.

WHITE SPIRITS SUITED TO A HARD SHAKE

Generally, white spirits can be said to go very well with fruit juices, which are difficult to mix with spirits. This makes a hard shake ideal for cocktails using fruit juices.

Gin

Gin is generally known to mix well with almost any other liquor. It has a very broad character, which is why it is the most commonly used white spirit in cocktail mixing. That doesn't mean gin has no character whatsoever. Gin has a unique light flavor that's created by distilling the base grain ingredients including barley and rye, and then redistilling this together with juniper berries and other botanicals. Gin has a character that stands very well on its own.

I use Gordon's for shaken cocktails because it has that unique gin flavor and aroma as well as a strong body. This powerful, simple gin blooms beautifully with a hard shake. I like to use Beefeater for stirred and built cocktails thanks to its sharp, urbane character.

Vodka

I use Smirnoff Red Label (80 proof) for its strength of character. There are vodkas with higher proofs, but Red Label provides more than enough bite when mixed into a cocktail.

Vodka is a grain-based distilled spirit that's filtered using birch charcoal. Therefore it has no characteristics whatsoever and can be mixed with any other ingredient, although it works particularly well with fresh fruit. It does this because it doesn't interfere with the flavor of the fruit; if anything, vodka only acts to boost the delicate flavor and aroma of the fruit with the power of its alcohol.

Another appeal of vodka is its ability to bring out the best in liqueurs. However, vodka can also increase sweetness. Therefore, when it's mixed with a liqueur, the proportion of the liqueur has to be reduced a bit. For example, take the gin-based White Lady, which is made with Cointreau and lemon juice, and the vodka-based Balalaika. The amount of Cointreau used in the Balalaika is slightly lower than what's used in the White Lady. Simply put, vodka doesn't have a character that calls attention to itself; instead, it provides a strong supporting role for whatever cocktail it is used in.

Rum

Rum is a sugar cane-based distilled liquor that comes in a white spirit type and a brown spirit type. You can tell by looking at them: one is colorless and transparent, and one has a golden or brown color due to a barrel-aging process.

There are three types of rum categorized by color: white rum (e.g., from Cuba or Puerto Rico); gold rum (e.g., from former French colonies in the Caribbean); and dark rum (e.g., from Jamaica). The flavors are divided into light, medium and heavy, although these do not necessarily correspond to the color. Only white rum is always light in flavor.

I use Bacardi, which is the most popular brand for use in cocktails. Bacardi's Cuban factory was the first to make light rum. Rum is another spirit that mixes well with others. That said, it has an impressive aftertaste when used in a cocktail, and that presence asserts itself.

Tequila

Tequila, a spirit made from a plant in the agavaceae family known as agave azul tequilana, has the strongest character of any of the four white spirits discussed here. Of the various brands, Sauza retains the original character of tequila and has a big-bodied flavor suitable for a hard shake.

Like rum, tequila also comes in a barrel-aged yellow variety. Tequila labeled reposado has been aged more than two months while añejo indicates aging of more than one year. Añejo tequilas retain the aroma of the barrel and have a fuller body, although this means that the unique strength and aroma of the tequila are reduced.

BROWN SPIRITS

HEART AND SOUL—BROWN SPIRITS

Whiskey and brandy are the most common brown spirits, and they have a unique flavor and aroma that can be enjoyed on their own. Since these liquors have such strong personalities, the question becomes, "How do we use them in cocktails?" In search of the answer, we'll turn our attention first to mettle-testing shaken cocktails that use a brown-spirit base.

A brown spirit is any barrel-aged distilled liquor that has an amber color. A unique aroma characterizes these liquors. Whiskey, brandy and dark rum are the brown spirits most commonly used in cocktails, and these three liquors can be further divided according to the ingredients and manufacturing processes used.

Whiskey comes in Scotch, Irish, Bourbon, Canadian (rye) and Japanese varieties. Brandy is divided into grape brandy (cognac, armagnac) and fruit brandies (leaving out, for this discussion, clear brandies). Flavors and prices vary, even within the same brand, according to the age and grade of the liquor.

So, why are there so many more cocktails that use white spirits rather than brown if the latter come in such a wide variety and are so widely drunk? The art of mixing cocktails involves creating a flavor that is greater than the sum of the parts. Because brown spirits are such complete liquors in and of themselves, it is extremely difficult to bring out something more from them. Of course, that difficulty can be viewed as a challenge when you consider defining the art of making cocktails. In this sense, cocktails that use brown spirits as a base could be called the heart and soul of cocktail mixing.

SCOTCH WHISKEY'S UNIQUE FLAVOR

Scotch whiskey is whiskey produced in Scotland. It comes in three types: malt whiskey made from malted barley, grain whiskey made from malted barley and grain, and blended whiskey made from a blend of malt and grain whiskeys.

The most popular type of scotch whiskey right now is blended whiskey (which I will just refer to as *scotch*), because the grain takes the edge off the very powerful malt. Indeed, you might almost call blended whiskey a cocktail in and of itself. It is very difficult to use this kind of blended liquor with a hard shake; however, since this technique first involves breaking down the flavor and then putting it back together. Also, by shaking scotch you bring out a bitterness that isn't present in the scotch alone. This bitterness gets in the way of the flavor of a cocktail. Stirring and building are therefore better options when using scotch.

The King's Valley is one of my own creations, and it uses scotch whiskey, Cointreau, lime juice and blue curaçao. I use one of two types of scotch in this cocktail, Whyte & McKay or Old Parr.

Whyte & McKay has a less prominent scotch flavor and therefore doesn't develop the bitterness that detracts from a cocktail. Old Parr, on the other hand, retains a unique scotch power but doesn't become bitter. It therefore creates a flavor appropriate to whiskey-base cocktails. I choose this one for guests who like scotch.

Malt scotch is made with malted barley only and is made differently than other kinds of scotch. It might actually be a better fit for cocktails than blended whiskeys, but it's extremely expensive, which in practice means you're better off drinking it by itself.

THE CHARM OF BOURBON

The type of whiskey that is most suited to a hard shake is without doubt bourbon with its smoky, muddy strength. The strongest bourbon is Old Grand-Dad, but since the shape of the bottle has recently changed to one that is difficult to handle, I've been using Beam's Choice 8-year old instead.

Bourbon is very good in whiskey cocktails like a Whiskey Sour or a New York. The most important thing when making a cocktail using any brown spirit (not just bourbon) is to find a good balance among the ingredients in terms of sourness (lemons or limes) and sweetness (syrups), thereby controlling a bit of the *orneriness* of the whiskey.

GRAPE BRANDY AND APPLE BRANDY

The most popular kinds of grape brandy are cognac and armagnac. I use Hennessey VS (cognac), which has a strong enough character to work well with a hard shake. Very aromatic brandies like VSOP tend to be weaker, but I do use VSOP in stirred cocktails because of its elaborate fragrance.

One popular fruit brandy used in brown spirit cocktails is apple brandy, which is made by fermenting apple juice and then distilling the cider. The standard recipe for a Jack Rose, which is made with lime juice and grenadine, calls for an American apple brandy called applejack, but I prefer calvados, which is made in the Normandy region of France and has a fuller flavor. I reduce the amount of grenadine, compensate with a bit of sugar syrup and establish a good balance between the tart and the sweet components, which results in a light Daiquiri-type cocktail.

HOW TO DRINK DARK RUM

Dark rum, a barrel-aged rum made from molasses, has a dense, full-bodied flavor. Jamaican rum such as Myer's Rum is probably the most famous. It is often drunk on the rocks or straight but is also used as an ingredient in hot cocktails such as a Hot Buttered Rum or a Hot Rum Cow.

WHISKEY COMPATIBILITIES IN COCKTAILS

S = Scotch, I = Irish, B = Bourbon, C = Canadian, J = Japanese
3 = Compatible, 2 = Moderately Compatible, 1 = Incompatible

Cocktail	S	I	B	C	J	Remarks
Manhattan	1	1	2	3	1	Rye whiskey works well. (Canadian whiskey is made from rye.)
Rob Roy	3	1	1	1	1	Also called a Scotch Manhattan—a Manhattan made with scotch.
Whiskey Sour	2	2	3	2	2	Made with bourbon in the US and scotch in Europe.
New York	1	1	3	2	1	What else but bourbon?
Old-Fashioned	2	2	3	2	2	Some recipes call for Canadian.
Irish Coffee	1	3	1	1	1	It's in the name.
Godfather	3	2	2	2	2	A variation on the Rusty Nail, so scotch, but Canadian also works.
Rusty Nail	3	2	1	2	2	Because it includes Drambuie, a liqueur made from scotch.
Mint Julep	1	1	3	1	1	It's a cocktail invented in Kentucky, after all.
Four-Leaf Clover	1	1	1	1	3	Won top honors at a Suntory competition.
King's Valley	3	1	1	1	1	Won an award at a cocktail competition hosted by the Scotch Whiskey Association.
Moon River	1	1	3	1	1	Created in the spirit of *Breakfast at Tiffany's*.

Source: Kazuo Uyeda, *Cocktails*, Seitosha

LIQUEURS

THE CHARM OF LIQUEURS

In recent years, a surprising number of cocktails have been winning awards in Japanese cocktail competitions using a liqueur as a base or in which the base spirit has been reduced to one-third and the proportion of liqueur has been increased. The trick in making these cocktails is to avoid a cloying sweetness by using fruit juice to achieve a lighter flavor.

Recently a lychee liqueur called Dita (Soho) has become very popular among young women in Japan. The strong character of this liqueur is well matched by citrus fruit juices. When these two trends are looked at together, the overall picture that emerges is one of lower alcohol content in cocktails.

If, in the past, a guest requested a cocktail with lower alcohol content the simplest solution would be to use a liqueur, which increased the sweetness. However, a low-alcohol drink without the sweetness is a bartender's worst nightmare. Because of this, full-bodied liqueurs like Peachtree have garnered a lot of attention, since they do not have that cloying sweetness of other liqueurs.

These drinks are generally made with a white spirit base together with a light-colored strawberry, apricot, lychee or watermelon liqueur mixed with some kind of citrus juice and then shaken and poured over ice in a rocks glass.

Liqueurs have a long history as medicinal drinks, as is the case with Bénédictine and Chartreuse. Since the trend today is for lower alcohol content, one way of enjoying dense liqueurs is to pour them into a small glass and have them as an after-dinner digestif. They are also good as apéritifs when mixed with soda.

WHAT LIQUEURS ARE AND HOW THEY ARE MADE

Liqueurs are made all over the world today. In Japan we have green tea liqueurs as well as Midori and Sakura, and these are enjoyed in all countries. However, there is no universal definition of what constitutes a liqueur. Essentially, most liqueurs are a distilled alcohol with the addition of some kind of aromatic flavoring as well as a sweetener and coloring.

Japanese liqueurs belong to a category known as *mixed liquors*, which includes not only liqueurs made from distilled alcohol, but also certain types of wine-based drinks like vermouth which are fermented.

Let's take a closer look at how liqueurs are made. Start with the basic ingredient, which is the distilled alcohol. This is generally a neutral spirit (any alcohol which has been distilled to an alcoholic content of 95% or more). Both white and brown spirits are used.

Next comes the flavoring, which comes in four types: 1) herbs/spices 2) fruit 3) nuts/seeds/grains and 4) other. The flavoring can be added in many different ways, but there are three general methods: distilling, immersion and essence. Simply put, these methods involve, respectively, adding the flavoring component to the base spirit and then distilling it, immersing the ingredient of the flavoring component inside the spirit or adding a concentrated essence of the flavoring to the spirit.

The sweetener and coloring agent are added to this, and, depending on the specific liqueur, water may also be added.

CHARACTERISTICS OF LIQUEURS

Liqueurs are sweet and characterized by unique flavors, colors and aromas. The color is an important factor, since a beautiful color can add a great deal to the flavor. The sweetness of liqueur allows them to be used as a substitute for sweeteners such as sugar syrup.

There exists a kind of liqueur known as a crème liqueur. Crème liqueurs are so named for their smooth consistency, since they contain more extract than base alcohol (although in practice there are no strict criteria for defining the various types).

SELECTING LIQUEURS

It would be impossible to collect one of each kind of liqueur, but there are a few standards that every bar should keep handy. Some liqueurs are available in different brands. While it may be hard to choose one, the choice is ultimately a matter of preference. I tend to stick to a brand that is known for one type of liqueur, e.g., Cointreau for white curaçao and Grand Marnier for orange curaçao. Of course that's not to say that some larger manufacturers don't produce some fine liqueurs, and I use quite a few of them, too.

The defining characteristics of any liqueur are its flavor and color. When making an original cocktail, it is often necessary to specify a brand to achieve the desired color and flavor.

Another important element in selecting a liqueur is how long the liqueur holds its flavor after the seal is broken. Liqueurs are used in smaller quantities than spirits, which means that some clear liqueurs can start fogging in as little as two months. Color is of the utmost importance in cocktails, so you always have to check the color of the liqueurs you are using. Keep in mind that you have to wipe the mouth of the bottle after use; otherwise it can crust over with sugar.

TOOLS

SHAKER VS. MIXING GLASS

While the US is believed to be birthplace of the cocktail made with ice (thanks to a quick and early embrace of Linde's invention of the ice-making machine), one important question remains. Was the first cocktail shaken or stirred?

The first edition of the *Savoy Cocktail Book* (a cocktail recipe book published in 1930 by London's Savoy Hotel with recipes compiled by Harry Craddock of the Savoy's American Bar) states that a Martini should be shaken. However, a few editions later the author changes his mind and says it should be stirred. Consider this in the light of Agent 007's famous request ("shaken, not stirred"), and the evidence seems to point towards the shaker coming before the mixing glass. Indeed, stirring could have been developed later, as a simpler way to mix ingredients.

TYPES AND USES OF SHAKERS

Broadly speaking, shakers come in two types: those with internal strainers and those without them. The internal strainer type is common in Japan, but the opposite is true in Europe and the US. A Boston shaker doesn't have an internal strainer but instead consists of a main glass into which a smaller glass is placed. Some speculate that this simple construction is the origin of the shaker, which was then further developed to include the internal strainer as an aid in pouring. This also might be why the bottom glass is used as a mixing glass. Also, at one time, there were shakers with spouts.

CHOOSING A SHAKER

Let's take a practical look at shakers with internal strainers beginning with the construction material. The easiest material to use and take care of is stainless steel. It's tough and can be cleaned easily with a sponge and water or a neutral detergent.

If you're a professional bartender, however, you'll probably want a nickel silver shaker. Its advantage over stainless steel is that it chills faster.

Also, the ice makes a beautiful sound in it – slightly but distinctly different from the sound of stainless steel.

Nickel silver shakers are cleaned the same way that stainless steel shakers are, and any tarnish can be removed using ordinary silver polish (cream or liquid). I can't really recommend pure silver shakers because they're too soft.

The major difference between stainless steel shakers and nickel silver shakers is the shape. Typically, stainless steel shakers have rounded bodies while nickel silver shakers are straighter. When shaking a cocktail, the roundness aids the rotation of the ice and therefore improves mixing, which you'll agree is important. To compensate for the differences, some bartenders use different shakers for different cocktails.

Now, regarding sizes: for a hard shake, there has to be a lot more ice than ingredients in the shaker, so I use a three-serving shaker when making one cocktail.

Another important factor is the size of the holes in the strainer. The fine shards of ice created by the hard shake have to come out through these holes, and the size and number varies by shaker. I prefer strainers with bigger holes. If two shakers have strainers with the same size holes, then I pick the one that has more.

CHOOSING A MIXING GLASS

A mixing glass should be made from thick, solid glass. This prevents the surrounding air temperature and the heat from your fingers from being transmitted to the ingredients inside. Unlike shakers, mixing glasses do not need to be very big, although a certain size allows you greater freedom of use.

In past competitions I used a mixing glass with a stem, and it was useful when making large quantities. The problem with very large mixing glasses, however, is that they are very big around and difficult to hold with one hand and, if they are very deep, it's difficult to stir the ingredients inside. Therefore, I decided on a mixing glass that I could comfortably hold at the bottom with one hand but was still large and easy to pour. The shape of the pouring lip varies from glass to glass, so you should try out several and pick one that doesn't dribble.

Shakers with internal strainers. The most popular shape is to the far right. One option is to use a nickel silver shaker for short drinks that you want to chill rapidly and a stainless steel one for long drinks that are bigger and more difficult to mix. Choose a thicker shaker if you're going to go with stainless steel because this transmits less heat.

Mixing glasses. The one on the right has a stem and can make up to five servings at once. The wide body allows for greater (and more graceful) movement of the barspoon. The glass to the left is more typical and can make up to three servings. In front is the strainer. Strainers with a cut-out for pouring are for Boston shakers, which do not have a pouring lip. Strainers without the cut-out are typically easier to use for pouring.

Shakers without internal strainers generally come in two parts. The one to the right is a Boston shaker, which has a glass body that can be used as a mixing glass as well. To the left is a shaker that only has a top and a body but is shaped like a shaker with an internal strainer.

Two barspoons, a sommelier's knife and three jiggers. Barspoons are used with an extended tip to prevent damage to ice while mixing. Nickel silver barspoons are better than stainless steel ones because of their heft as well as their beautiful finish. Choose one that best fits your hand. The jigger on the left is the kind that is popular in Japan, while the others are popular in Europe.

COCKTAIL GLASSES

AN ESSENTIAL ELEMENT FOR A GOOD COCKTAIL

The glass is a very important element in the cocktail experience. The feeling of a particular cocktail can be radically transformed by changing the glass in which it's served. Some recipes call for specific glasses.

Unquestionably, cocktail glasses are a way of enhancing and beautifying the contents of a cocktail. The cocktail itself is naturally the star of the show, but the cocktail glass plays a very important supporting role that should never be overlooked. Picking the right glass is also a reflection of the bartender's character and philosophy.

This is how I pick glasses. Generally, I go for something relatively simple with fewer cuts and less decoration on the body so that the color of the cocktail, the bubbles and the thin shards of ice are clearly visible. I think it's best to avoid anything too elaborate because it upstages the drink.

Something else that adds to the flavor of the cocktail is thin glass, which guests often prefer.

But the most important thing is for the bartender to have a solid image of what the cocktail is. For example, I serve a Martini in a glass that is broad and slightly curved, but I serve a Daiquiri in a glass with straighter, sharper lines. I think having an image of what glass to serve a cocktail in translates into better cocktails.

So what kinds of glasses are out there? Let's take a look at some basic types.

ROUNDED COCKTAIL GLASSES

Glasses with a bit of curve are good for sweeter cocktails. The glass second from the left has a frosted Japanese-style pattern cut into it, so I use this one for cocktails with Japanese names or that use Japanese ingredients. I use the one in the middle for Manhattans, and the one to the right of that for Sidecars. The one all the way to the right is an all-purpose glass.

TRIANGULAR COCKTAIL GLASSES

I use glass with this kind of sharp form for drier cocktails. I use the one on the far left for Bamboos and Adonises. The two next to it are all-round glasses, which I use for Daiquiris and similar drinks. The tall, slim glasses are good for cocktails like Gibsons.

TUMBLERS

These glasses are for long drinks. From the left: a tumbler with a handle for hot drinks, a Collins glass that is slightly taller than a tumbler, a pilsner glass that is good for cocktails with fruit juice, and the last two are tumblers. I use the straight one for cocktails while the rounded one adds a touch of class to drinks that aren't mixed.

ROCKS GLASSES

Rocks glasses also come in many shapes: straight, flared, rounded, and so on. I use this type of glass for drinks served on the rocks as well as rocks-style drinks like Kamikazes, Charlie Chaplins, Sea Breezes, etc.

WINE GLASSES

From the left: for both white and red wine. You can also use these for Daisies, Fixes, and so on. The other two are champagne glasses. The shorter one is good for classic cocktails like Champagne Cocktails and Pink Ladies. I use the beautiful fluted one for Kir Royals, Mimosas, etc.

STANDARD COCKTAILS

- All ingredients (except spirits) and glasses should be chilled in a refrigerator ahead of time unless otherwise noted.
- As described in the previous section, but omitted from the descriptions in this section, ice should be placed in the shaker or mixing glass before shaking or stirring.
- In the listing of ingredients, parentheses indicate brand names. In the instructions, parentheses indicate types of liquors.
- The above also applies to the later section of original cocktails.

GIN-BASE STANDARD COCKTAILS

MARTINI

In the postwar years since cocktails were introduced to Japan, the Martini has been the hands-down number one most popular cocktail of all the hundreds of mixed drinks available. Many people are very particular about their Martinis. And not just drinkers—many bartenders use this transparent liquid as a vehicle of philosophical expression. What is the appeal of the Martini, and why can it incite such heated debate?

The unique flavor of the main ingredient might go a long way to explaining the popularity of this drink. Since the Martini is a simple combination of gin and dry vermouth, the drinker can, in a sense, participate in the creation of the flavor. I think this is the main reason why Martinis are so popular.

This also explains why there are so many recipes. The most commonly used basic ingredients are 1) dry gin 2) dry vermouth 3) bitters 4) olives and 5) lemon peel. There exist eight Martini recipes using these ingredients. In addition, it is possible to create variations by changing the proportions and the combinations. And, when you include the different brands of liquors that can be used, the resulting number of variations is almost infinite.

Martinis are also a sensitive indicator of social trends, e.g., Martinis tend to become extremely dry as the general taste leans towards drier cocktails.

The Gin & It, the drink on which the Martini is based, is made with gin and sweet vermouth in a 1:1 ratio. The Martini was born when the sweet vermouth was replaced with dry vermouth. The ratio was initially 2:1. In contrast to this, the Dry Martini had a ratio of 3:1. They existed as different cocktails, clearly defined from one another.

As the preference for dryness grew, the distinction between a Martini and a Dry Martini became blurred. The latter gradually became the former, and the ratio became even more disproportionate. Eventually, you started getting recipes which called for a ratio of 20:1—just a spray of dry vermouth or a rinse (i.e., pouring the vermouth into the mixing glass with ice, stirring it, then pouring out the vermouth and pouring in the gin and stirring it with the *vermouth-rinsed* ice). Some people were satisfied merely to sip straight gin and tip their glass in the direction of a vermouth bottle.

You can find bars that will serve this kind of thing and call it a Martini, but that's not for me. You can only call a drink a Martini when the gin and the dry vermouth are mixed together to create a new flavor that lacks the stimulating sensation of the gin. In other words, Martinis are not some kind of science experiment designed to maximize the flavor of the gin. I place the outer limits to the proportions of the ratio at 6:1 (or maybe 7:1, if I'm feeling magnanimous that day). As it turns out, the taste for dry cocktails in general seems to be returning to earth bit by bit.

It goes without saying that the most important aspect of making a Martini is the stirring technique. No cocktail brings home the difficulty of stirring better than a Martini. There is no shortcut to making a good Martini. You just have to focus your mind on the mixing and really put your heart into it. And, you have to repeat this over and over. Also, you mustn't forget the correct method for garnishing the lemon peel as the finishing touch.

Standard Recipe

3 parts dry gin
1 part dry vermouth

Uyeda Recipe

5 parts dry gin (Beefeater)
1 part dry vermouth (Noilly Prat)
1 stuffed olive
Lemon peel

Glass: cocktail glass

Stir the dry gin and dry vermouth in a mixing glass. Serve in a cocktail glass and garnish with a lemon peel and a stuffed olive on a cocktail spear.

Dry vermouth. Noilly Prat on the right and Martini Extra Dry on the left. The Noilly Prat is visibly darker and has a sweeter flavor.

Martini ingredients and possible combinations:

Ingredients	Combinations
1) Dry gin	A. 1+2
2) Dry vermouth	B. 1+2+3
3) Bitters	C. 1+2+4
4) Stuffed olives	D. 1+2+5
5) Lemon peel	E. 1+2+3+4
	F. 1+2+3+5
	G. 1+2+4+5
	H. 1+2+3+4+5

GIN-BASE STANDARD COCKTAILS

GIBSON

Popular lure has it that this cocktail is named after Charles Dana Gibson, an illustrator who was popular at the beginning of the 20th century. Gibson was the creator of the famous *Gibson Girls*, a series of illustrations that epitomized the independent free-spirited American woman at that time.

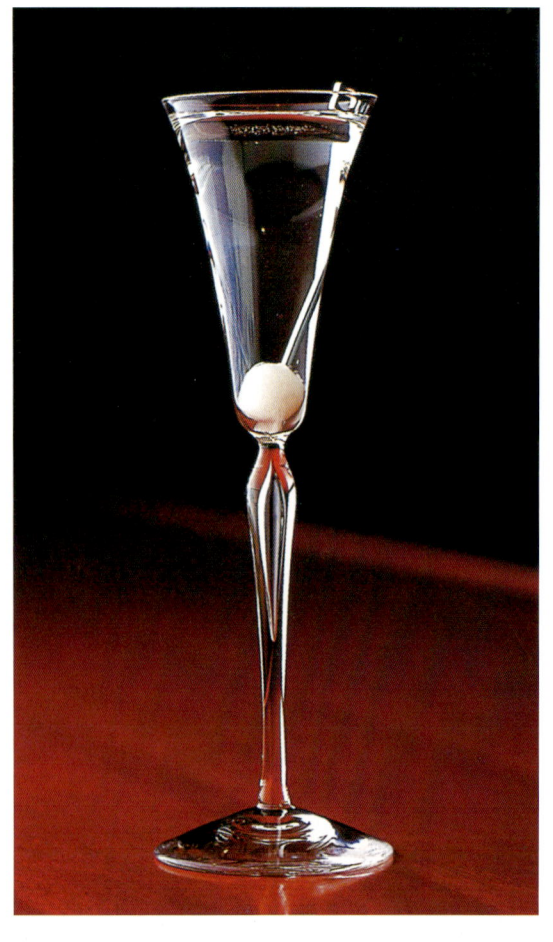

The first edition of the *Savoy Cocktail Book* states that a Gibson, like a Martini, should be shaken. But, as the drink's popularity spread, stirring became the norm, although occasionally you can still find a recipe that calls for shaking.

Initially, the Gibson was the paragon of the extremely dry cocktail. As dry Martinis became more and more popular, the Gibson was gradually sidelined. Today, the only actual difference between a Martini and a Gibson is that the former is garnished with an olive and the latter with a pearl onion.

That said, a Martini and a Gibson are cocktails that have totally different flavors. So, if the dryness of a Martini exceeds that of a Gibson, then there's no point in either cocktail. This is why I think a ratio of 5:1 is the limit for a Martini and 6:1 for a Gibson. I personally try to make a Gibson with more of a bite then a Martini.

A cocktail glass with a sharp silhouette is a perfect match for this sharp drink in honor of the slim and elegant *Gibson Girls*.

Standard Recipe

5 parts dry gin
1 part dry vermouth
1 pearl onion

Uyeda Recipe

6 parts dry gin (Beefeater)
1 part dry vermouth (Noilly Prat)
1 pearl onion

Glass: cocktail glass

Stir the dry gin and dry vermouth in a mixing glass. Pour into a cocktail glass and garnish with a pearl onion on a cocktail spear.

GIMLET

A round piece of ice floating in the middle of a large champagne coupe surrounded by fine shards of ice: this is the Gimlet I make using a hard shake. Putting ice in a champagne glass is the Tokyo Kaikan style. Gimlets were once made at Tokyo Kaikan with sugar around the rim of a champagne coupe, the choice of glass made in order to make the presentation more beautiful. Due to the size of the mouth of the glass, the

> **Lime juice cordials.** Rose's on the right and Meijiya on the left. Both are sweetened syrups.

bartender would put a single piece of ice inside to keep the drink cool.

When bartenders first began decorating the rims of glasses in Japan (in the 1950s), they almost always used sugar, perhaps because sweet things were still a luxury in the immediate postwar period. Examples include the Kiss of Fire and My Tokyo. As the years passed, cocktails were made less sweet, and eventually the Gimlet with the sugar encrusted rim disappeared. All that's left is the champagne glass.

The Gimlet that I make uses fresh lime juice instead of a lime cordial (a kind of sweetened syrup). Whoever invented this cocktail probably used a cordial as a substitute for fresh lime juice. Today fresh limes aren't hard to get, so I don't think there's any reason not to use them instead of the cordial.

I use sugar syrup to add sweetness. In cocktails that use fruit juices, no matter how dry the trends may be, the optimum balance of spirit to fruit juice is 3:1. One teaspoon of sugar syrup balances the sweetness and the sourness, creating the flavor of the Gimlet.

In recent years I've seen something called a Dry Gimlet that doesn't use sugar, but I think it's safe to say that whatever the drink may be, it isn't a Gimlet.

Standard Recipe
3 parts dry gin
1 part lime juice cordial

Uyeda Recipe
3 parts dry gin (Gordon's)
1 part fresh lime juice
1 teaspoon sugar syrup

Glass: champagne coupe

Shake the dry gin, fresh lime juice and sugar syrup in a shaker. Serve in a champagne coupe together with a single piece of ice.

GIN-BASE STANDARD COCKTAILS

ALASKA

アラスカ

The Alaska, in order to mix and chill the ingredients, was originally a shaken cocktail, but one of the characteristics of my hard shake is introducing bubbles into the mixture and rounding out the flavor. In cocktails like the Alaska, the Stinger and the Russian, which are put together without fruit juices or creams and only use the base spirit together with a sweetener, it's very difficult to include the bubbles using a hard shake, because they disappear quickly.

I therefore got the idea of stirring instead of shaking these cocktails, and that's exactly what I recommend in this book. I changed the original ratio of dry gin to Chartreuse from 3:1 to 5:1, successfully making it drier for stirring. The powerful sweetness of the Chartreuse is controlled, creating a sharper flavor overall, but the unique aroma of the Chartreuse remains. In this case, stirring is the perfect way to blend the two unique characters of the ingredients.

The only problem is that you can chill ingredients much better by shaking them. It is called an Alaska, after all, so it would be appropriate to shake it until condensation appeared on the outside of the shaker. So, you have two options: stir for flavor or shake for image. Indeed, you could shake it if the guest wants that. If you do, however, then the limit on the dryness is probably 4:1.

If you use a green Chartreuse, then you have a Green Alaska.

Standard Recipe	Uyeda Recipe
3 parts dry gin	5 parts dry gin (Beefeater)
1 part yellow Chartreuse	1 part yellow Chartreuse

Glass: cocktail glass

Stir the dry gin and yellow Chartreuse in a mixing glass and pour into a cocktail glass.

GIN & BITTERS

Chill the gin in the freezer and not the refrigerator for this cocktail, since the purpose is to enjoy the flavor of the gin itself. This is also why you should ask if the guest has a preference for a brand of gin.

Because this cocktail has a long history, there are many variations. The most common way of serving it used to be on the rocks. Today you can find it served in a cocktail or a sherry glass. I use a shot glass with a stem. No matter what kind of glass you use though, the glass should be thoroughly chilled beforehand.

There are many ways to mix a Gin & Bitters. The standard recipe calls for 2-3 dashes of bitters to be put in a glass and then poured out, after which the gin is added. Sometimes it's stirred, but since freezers are very common, there is no need to chill the gin by stirring.

I start by placing three drops of bitters in a chilled shot glass that has a stem, and then pour in dry gin that has been chilled to a very low temperature. I then add two more drops of bitters. By adding two or three drops before and after the gin, the bitters mix naturally and create a wonderful flavor.

This cocktail is also called a Pink Gin. Replace the Angostura bitters with orange bitters, it becomes a Yellow Gin.

Standard Recipe	Uyeda Recipe
1 glass of dry gin	1 glass of dry gin
2-3 dashes of Angostura bitters	5 drops of Angostura bitters

Glass: shot glass (with stem)

Put three drops of Angostura bitters in a shot glass. Add dry gin that has been chilled in the freezer. Add another two drops of Angostura bitters.

GIN & TONIC

This is one of the simplest recipes there is: gin and tonic water. It's a refreshingly light drink and, of all the built cocktails, the Gin & Tonic is probably the most popular cocktail in the world.

However, the simplest cocktails can be the trickiest. If you mix this cocktail wrong, the flavor will be flat and dull, but, if you do it right, it will retain its freshness and power to the last drop.

The most important factor affecting this difference is your approach to the technique of building. People often think that building a cocktail merely involves pouring the ingredients directly into the glass. However, only if you understand what's most important in this simple action can you make a delicious Gin & Tonic.

First of all, let's look at the tonic water. A light, refreshing flavor is obviously very important in a Gin & Tonic, and to retain that flavor and the carbonation, the tonic water must be poured gently, avoiding hitting the ice directly. The amount of tonic water to use is also very tricky. Use too much, the cocktail becomes watery. In my opinion, no more than 2 ounces should be used.

The next thing to consider is chilling the base liquor. Chilling reduces the risk of the cocktail becoming watery. I recommend this only as a safety measure. Finally, I add fresh lime to lighten the flavor.

Make this cocktail with one thought in your head: that you want the drink to be as cool and refreshing at the last sip as it is at the first sip. If you don't, the result won't taste good.

Finally, a note about brands of dry gin. I use Beefeater for its balanced flavor, but Tanqueray has a lighter finish, whereas Gordon's brings a richer aroma and sweetness to a cocktail. Using Bombay Sapphire will result in a Gin & Tonic with a more concentrated flavor that's not quite like the others.

Standard Recipe	Uyeda Recipe
1 1/2 ounce dry gin Tonic water	1 1/2 ounce dry gin (Beefeater) Tonic water 1/6 slice of lime (about 1/8 ounce of juice)

Glass: tumbler

Squeeze the slice of lime into a tumbler and then drop in the slice. Pour in the gin and then—very gently—the tonic water, and stir slowly. Add fresh lime juice if the flavor is too sweet.

GIN-BASE STANDARD COCKTAILS

WHITE LADY

ホワイト・レディ

The White Lady is a Sidecar-type cocktail. In fact, the Sidecar is just a White Lady with brandy instead of gin as the base, so it's actually more accurate to say that the Sidecar is a variation of a White Lady. In time the Sidecar became more popular and eventually came to be seen as a standard. Indeed, today the tables have been turned, and you can even hear the White Lady called a Gin Sidecar.

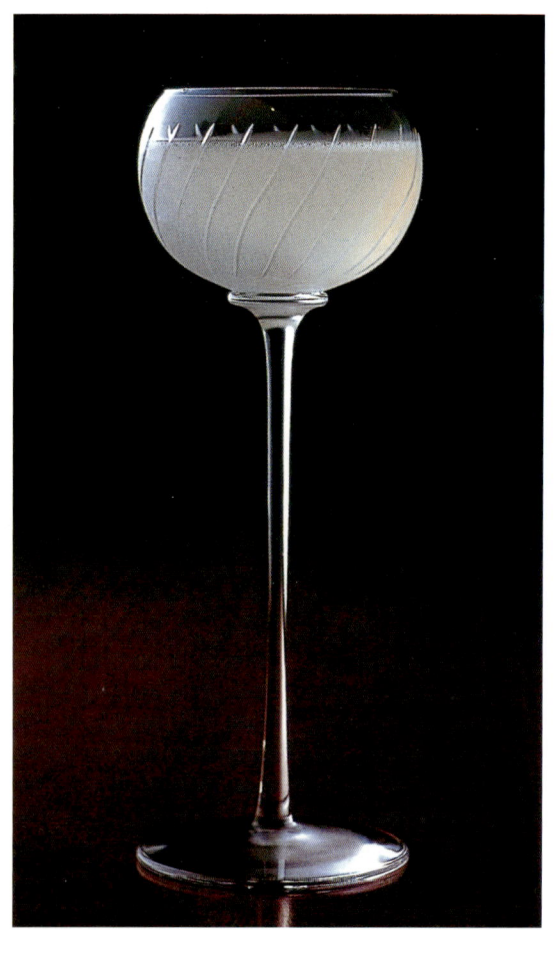

My recipe uses a hard shake and therefore the proportions of Cointreau and fresh lemon juice are lower than the standard recipe. Since the sweetness of the Cointreau has been limited in order to bring out a lighter flavor, the fresh lemon juice has also been reduced to match the reduced sweetness. Even if the guest wants a drier White Lady, this balance must be maintained. If the sweetness is reduced, the sourness must also be reduced.

The beautiful white appearance fits the name of the cocktail perfectly. I recommend a glass with soft, feminine curves.

The White Lady has a sister cocktail called a Pink Lady which uses grenadine and egg whites instead of the Cointreau. This has led some bartenders to add egg whites to a White Lady, but, in my view, this just eliminates the freshness that defines the flavor for me. It's that freshness that I aim for.

Standard Recipe	Uyeda Recipe
2 parts dry gin	4 parts dry gin (Gordon's)
1 part white curaçao	1 part Cointreau
1 part lemon juice	1 part fresh lemon juice

Glass: cocktail glass

Shake the dry gin, Cointreau (white curaçao) and fresh lemon juice in a shaker. Serve in a cocktail glass.

GIMLET HIGHBALL　ギムレット・ハイボール

This is a highball made by adding soda to a Gimlet. The term highball used to mean a drink that included any carbonated ingredient, including ginger ale and tonic water, and not just soda water. Under this definition, a Gin & Tonic is a type of highball. In Japan, the most popular highball is a Whiskey Highball, which is simply whiskey mixed with soda water. A lot of people seem to think that this is the only kind of highball.

Since highball-style cocktails are made using a carbonated ingredient, you can't cut corners with the short drink acting as the base. In other words, you have to shake the base Gimlet so that there is a layer of fine shards of ice, just as you would otherwise. Since you will be adding carbonation, it's important to up the sweetness and add a bit of volume.

This drink is a reworking of the Gin Fizz, replacing the lemon with lime and reducing the amount of sugar syrup used. The result is a refreshing cocktail, one of the most popular in my bar. The retro-sounding name also has a nice touch.

Other highball-style cocktails include the Amer Picon Highball and two variations on the Whiskey Highball: the Bourbon Highball and the Rye Highball.

Standard Recipe
- 1 1/2 ounce dry gin
- 1/2 ounce lime juice
- 1 teaspoon powdered (confectioner's) sugar
- Soda

Uyeda Recipe
- 1 1/2 ounce dry gin (Gordon's)
- 1/2 ounce fresh lime juice
- 1 1/2 ounce sugar syrup
- Soda

Glass: tumbler

Shake the dry gin, fresh lime juice and sugar syrup in a shaker and pour into a tumbler. Add ice and soda.

BRANDY-BASE STANDARD COCKTAILS

SIDECAR   サイドカー

While there are many other cocktails that have the same sweetness/sourness balance, the Sidecar is one of the basic short cocktails made in a shaker. I call cocktails that have the same ratio of liquor, sweetness and sourness *Sidecar-type cocktails*.

The standard recipe calls for 2:1, but I make mine a bit drier, at 4:1. This ratio is the limit of dryness at which the balance of flavors can be maintained using a hard shake.

If you change the balance of the flavors, then you need to reduce the sweetness and the sourness by equal amounts. This is an iron rule in cocktail mixing. If you only change one, the balance is lost. For guests who like their cocktails on the dry side, I can go as far as using $1\frac{1}{3}$ ounce of cognac, a little under $\frac{1}{3}$ ounce of Cointreau and a little over $\frac{1}{3}$ ounce of lemon juice. Extremely dry recipes also exist; these use lemon juice and Cointreau in very small quantities, simply to add a bit of an atmosphere. However, the unique flavor of a Sidecar is lost, and such cocktails should be called by other names.

Naturally, many variations are possible in Sidecar-type cocktails (i.e., cocktails that use this 2:1 ratio), variations not only in the sweet and sour ingredients but also the base liquor. For example, you can combine two sweet ingredients such as grenadine and sugar syrup or combine two sour ingredients.

You should be fine when creating original cocktails or varying standard recipes as long as you don't change the 4:1 ratio. Obviously, since there are differences in the degree of sweetness and sourness with different ingredients, you have to adjust accordingly, but this is where your skill as a bartender is tested.

Standard Recipe
2 parts brandy
1 part white curaçao
1 part lemon juice

Uyeda Recipe
4 parts cognac (Hennessy VS)
1 part Cointreau
1 part fresh lemon juice

Glass: cocktail glass

Shake the cognac, Cointreau (white curaçao) and fresh lemon juice. Serve in a cocktail glass.

STINGER

The Stinger is a made by combining a spirit with a sweet ingredient. No fruit juice is used. Like the Alaska, the Stinger was originally shaken with the goal of quickly cooling the ingredients and thoroughly mixing them. However, after I perfected the hard shake, I realized that shaking was best suited to achieve a complete mix for hard-to-mix ingredients (like fruit juices and creams) and introducing bubbles to soften the flavor.

Accordingly, while cocktails made from ingredients that are fairly easy to mix (such as spirits and sweeteners) taste basically the same with or without a hard shake and they can't maintain the bubbles. In other words, these cocktails are not suited to the hard shake.

That's why I stir instead of shake the Stinger. Considering that Martinis used to be shaken and not stirred, I don't see a problem in stirring a Stinger. It may be unconventional, but I think it's worth it. The same can be said for replacing the cognac with vodka and making a Vodka Stinger.

I switched the base brandy from Hennessy VS to VSOP to emphasize that unique brandy flavor and use a 4:1 ratio to achieve a refreshing bite. Since stirring is a method that allows the personalities of each of the ingredients to shine through even if the sweetness is pulled back a bit, the character of the mint is not lost even at a dry 5:1 ratio, which I think is the limit.

The brandy and the mint mix beautifully.

Standard Recipe
2 parts brandy
1 part white crème de menthe

Uyeda Recipe
4 parts cognac (Hennessy VSOP)
1 part white crème de menthe (Get 31)

Glass: cocktail glass

Stir the cognac and white crème de menthe in a mixing glass and serve in a cocktail glass.

ALEXANDER　　　　　　　　　　アレキサンダー

This cocktail is named for Alexandra of Denmark, the Queen Consort to Edward VII. Like a Grasshopper, it uses fresh cream and, therefore, requires an extra long hard shake. I use more brandy than the standard recipe, however, so my recipe doesn't need to be shaken quite as long. Note that over-shaking causes the cream to separate and waters down the cocktail.

The Alexander is often drunk as a digestif. Freshly ground nutmeg was often sprinkled over the top in order to enhance the postprandial refreshment. When this cocktail was first introduced to Japan, the Japanese were not accustomed to the smell of fresh cream, and the nutmeg acted to conceal it. Today, this resistance to fresh cream is gone, and bartenders aim for a light, clean flavor with less sweetness and creaminess, obviating the need for nutmeg. In this Japanese bartenders are hardly alone: bartenders around the world hardly use nutmeg anymore either.

There are Alexander recipes that use equal proportions of brandy, crème de cacao and fresh cream, but contemporary trends show a preference for a drier recipe. I would say that the limit of dryness for the Alexander is 4:1:1.

Standard Recipe
2 parts brandy
1 part dark crème de cacao
1 part fresh cream

Uyeda Recipe
4 parts cognac (Hennessy VS)
1 part dark crème de cacao (De Kuyper)
1 part fresh cream

Glass: cocktail glass
Shake the cognac, crème de cacao and fresh cream in a shaker. Serve in a cocktail glass.

JACK ROSE

This cocktail, created in the US, uses an American apple brandy called applejack, perhaps the origin of the *Jack* portion of the name.

While the standard recipe calls for an extra helping of grenadine (providing the *Rose* portion of the name), which makes the Jack Rose a variation of the Sidecar. However, I think of this cocktail as a Daiquiri-type cocktail with a sour ingredient added to the base liquor. Therefore,

I reduce the proportion of grenadine and sharpen the flavor with fresh lime in order to bring out the tangy apple flavor.

I consider the grenadine more of a color additive than anything else. In order to highlight the bubbles that are created from the hard shake, I use sugar syrup instead to add the sweetness. The artificial flavor of the grenadine is also reduced, allowing the flavor of the calvados to come through.

The original recipe calls for applejack, but I find that calvados, which is an apple brandy from Normandy, has a much better flavor and aroma. So, that's what I use. Calvados varies a lot in price, depending on where and when it was made, and I prefer the higher-end Calvados Boulard, since it has the strength to hold up under a hard shake and has a wonderful bittersweet aroma that recalls the fragrance of roses.

Standard Recipe	Uyeda Recipe
2 parts applejack	3 parts calvados (Boulard, Grand Solage)
1 part lime juice	1 part fresh lime juice
1 part grenadine	1 teaspoon grenadine (Meijiya)
	1 teaspoon sugar syrup

Glass: cocktail glass

Shake the calvados, fresh lime juice, grenadine and sugar syrup in a shaker. Serve in a cocktail glass.

BRANDY SOUR

This is a sour-style cocktail, which means that sweet and sour elements are added to a spirit and shaken. The key to making a Brandy Sour is to bring out the sour flavor. There are two subtypes: English-style, in which a small amount of a carbonated ingredient (soda) is added, and American-style, which does without the carbonation. I prefer the American-style. Ordinary cocktails have a ratio of base spirit to sour ingredient of 3:1, but for sour-type cocktails, the proportion of fresh lemon juice is increased a bit and the sweetness is dialed down.

Since I use a hard shake on this cocktail, the brandy I use is Hennessy VS for the strength of its flavor. To achieve a clear color I use sugar syrup as a sweetener. Granulated sugar doesn't dissolve completely, and powdered sugar fogs the cocktail.

An orange slice or a maraschino cherry is typically used as a decoration, but I add one slice of a lemon and a single piece of ice. Sour-type cocktails are typically served in what are known as *sour glasses* (which hold 4 ounces), but a cocktail glass will do just fine.

Another type of popular sour cocktail is a Whiskey Sour, and one recent addition is an Aquavit Sour. You can also sometimes find sours that use liqueurs, but I don't really see the point in using a sweet liqueur in a sour-type cocktail.

Standard Recipe

- 1 1/2 ounce brandy
- 2/3 ounce lemon juice
- 1 teaspoon sugar
- 1 orange slice
- 1 maraschino cherry

Uyeda Recipe

- 1 1/2 ounce cognac (Hennessy VS)
- 2/3 ounce fresh lemon juice
- 1 teaspoon sugar syrup
- 1 lemon slice

Glass: sour glass

Shake the cognac, fresh lemon juice and sugar syrup in a shaker. Pour into a sour glass and add one piece of ice and the lemon slice.

WHISKEY-BASE STANDARD COCKTAILS

MANHATTAN　　　　　　　　　マンハッタン

This cocktail evokes the sun setting over Manhattan. The sweet vermouth adds the redness of the setting sun to the whiskey. It's said that Winston Churchill's American-born mother Jennie was an avid drinker of Manhattans in New York's Manhattan Club.

In the past, the Manhattan certainly enjoyed as much popularity as the queen of cocktails, the Martini, but this popularity has started to wane. Thanks to its storied history, however, there are many variations on the standard recipe. The most common include a Bourbon Manhattan that uses bourbon instead of rye, a Scotch Manhattan (a.k.a. Rob Roy) that uses scotch, and a Dry Manhattan that replaces the sweet vermouth with dry vermouth.

Like the Martini, the Manhattan has not escaped the trend towards dryness, and while standard recipe calls for ratio 3:1, I think that 4:1 is better with the upper limit being 5:1. If a guest wants an even drier Manhattan, I recommend a Dry Manhattan.

The upper limit on the Martini is 7:1, but the base liquor used in a Manhattan is different. While gin has a sharp flavor, whiskey has a brooding, complex character, which can easily overpower the other ingredients, so the limit is 5:1.

Focus on stirring evenly and gently. You're aiming for a soft flavor. Serve in a glass with soft, feminine curves.

Standard Recipe

3 parts rye
1 part sweet vermouth
1 dash of Angostura bitters
1 maraschino cherry
Lemon peel

Uyeda Recipe

4 parts rye (Alberta Springs 10 Year Old)
1 part sweet vermouth (Cinzano Rosso)
1 maraschino cherry
Lemon peel

Glass: cocktail glass

Stir the rye and sweet vermouth in a mixing glass. Serve in a cocktail glass with a maraschino cherry and the lemon peel for aroma.

NEW YORK

When you make this cocktail you'll witness a perfect example of the color changes characteristic of a hard shake. As the faint pink tone fills with tiny bubbles, it gradually takes on an orange hue.

The New York is a Daiquiri-type cocktail. The difficulty in making a New York is maintaining the balance between the sweet and sour components while controlling the unique character of the whiskey, which is extremely difficult to handle in shaken cocktails.

Some bartenders like to use rye (Canadian), but I choose bourbon, not just because the cocktail is named after an American city, but also because the bourbon works well with the sour ingredients and results in a nice, hefty finish.

The best type of bourbon for this cocktail is Old Grand-Dad with its powerful personality. The hard shake technique works best with ingredients that have this kind of heft.

Unlike some people who use a lot of grenadine to create a bright red New York, I use it to add just a touch of color and make up for the lack of sweetness with sugar syrup. The color and the sweetness are the two defining characteristics of this cocktail.

Note that some grenadine brands emphasize the flavor of pomegranate, but I prefer the Meijiya brand because it has the most beautiful color.

Standard Recipe
3 parts rye
1 part lime juice
1/2 teaspoon grenadine
1 teaspoon sugar
Orange peel

Uyeda Recipe
3 parts bourbon (Old Grand-Dad)
1 part fresh lime juice
1/2 teaspoon grenadine (Meijiya)
1 teaspoon sugar syrup

Glass: cocktail glass

Shake the bourbon, fresh lime juice, grenadine and sugar syrup in a shaker. Serve in a cocktail glass. Add an orange peel to taste.

OLD FASHIONED

As the name says, this is indeed a very old fashioned type of cocktail, even though it continues to be very popular today. Since the guest has a hand in adjusting the flavor to his or her tastes, your job is to provide the setup, being careful not to damage the flavor of the whiskey.

Typically, an Old Fashioned is served on the rocks with bitters and a single slice of lemon. No soda is used. However, in addition to the bitters, I add some soda to the sugar cubes to make them easier to dissolve and use crushed ice to give it a more modern look.

I use three types of fruit, which are a defining factor in the flavor, and cut each slice thick so the guest has more freedom to adjust the flavor. I cut the orange particularly thick, since it provides a lot of sweetness to the balance.

Finally, instead of a muddler, I serve the drink with a thin spoon, which is better for squeezing out the fruit juice.

Bourbon works best as the base whiskey because it mixes well with citrus flavors, but I let the guest choose the brand. There's a similar cocktail in France that calls for brandy instead of whiskey. Some people use dry gin or rum, as well.

Standard Recipe

- 1 1/2 ounce rye or bourbon
- 2 dashes of Angostura bitters
- 1 sugar cube
- 1 orange slice
- 1 lemon slice
- 1 maraschino cherry

Uyeda Recipe

- 1 1/2 ounces bourbon
- 1 sugar cube (small)
- 1 dash of Angostura bitters
- 2 dashes of soda
- 1 orange slice
- 1 lemon slice
- 1 lime slice

Glass: rocks glass (Old Fashioned glass)

Place the sugar cube into the glass and splash the Angostura bitters and soda over the sugar. Fill the glass about 5/8 to the top with crushed ice and add the bourbon. Insert the orange, lemon and lime slices between the side of the glass and the ice. Include a spoon.

VODKA-BASE STANDARD COCKTAILS

RUSSIAN ルシアン

Since this cocktail uses two base spirits, it has a high alcohol content, but the sweetness of the cacao makes it popular with women. The standard recipe calls for shaking, but I stir it.

Like the Alaska and the Stinger, the Russian only combines a spirit and a sweet ingredient, so it won't hold the bubbles produced by a hard shake. If there's no point in shaking it, then why not stir it in order to achieve a sharp flavor? By stirring it, the unique characters of the spirits can be brought out, even if the sweet crème de cacao is reduced by half.

The standard recipe uses equal amounts of each of the three ingredients, but if you stir the cocktail, then the balance changes. I increase the vodka and reduce the crème de cacao by a proportionate amount (because people prefer dry cocktails these days and because it's called a Russian, after all). When the proportion of base to sweet ingredient changes from 2:1 to 5:1, the result is a cleaner flavor with a relatively high alcohol content.

I recommend using a cocktail glass to bring out the soft depth of the sweetness of this drink. Incidentally, if you add fresh cream to the standard-recipe Russian, you get a Russian Bear.

Standard Recipe	Uyeda Recipe
1 part vodka	3 parts vodka (Smirnoff)
1 part dry gin	2 parts dry gin (Beefeater)
1 part dark crème de cacao	1 part dark crème de cacao (De Kuyper)

Glass: cocktail glass

Stir the vodka, dry gin and crème de cacao in a mixing glass. Serve in a cocktail glass.

SALTY DOG

This British cocktail was originally made with dry gin, but gin was replaced by vodka after the drink gained worldwide popularity. The light, fruity flavor appeals to people of all nations.

It's unknown whether the Margarita or the Salty Dog was the first drink to use a salt-encrusted rim, but it's said that Europeans aren't generally fond of this style, so you often see a *half-moon* style, in which salt is only applied to half of the rim. Incidentally, a Salty Dog without salt on the rim is called either a Bulldog or a Greyhound, since these breeds have short tails.

The defining ingredient is the grapefruit juice. Some bartenders use canned juice, and some mix canned juice with fresh juice. Others use fresh juice that has been left out overnight.

I prefer using freshly squeezed juice from white grapefruit, which provides a mild flavor and unrivaled fresh, fruity bouquet. The only problem with using fresh juice—and this makes it tricky to use—is that the flavor can vary considerably depending both on the season and the origin of the grapefruit. Since my job is ensuring that guests have the best possible cocktail drinking experience, I don't recommend this cocktail out of season.

The amount of fresh grapefruit juice used should be approximately double the amount of the base. Fresh juice has a very subtle flavor, which can easily become watery when the ice melts, so I use a single large piece of ice to prevent this.

Standard Recipe
1–1 1/2 ounce vodka
Grapefruit juice

Uyeda Recipe
1 1/2 ounce vodka (Smirnoff)
Fresh grapefruit juice

Glass: rocks glass (not chilled)
Place one large piece of ice in a rocks glass with sugar around the rim and add the vodka and fresh grapefruit juice. Stir lightly.

MOSCOW MULE

A copper serving mug adds a touch of interest to a Moscow Mule. The mug was originally a marketing tool by Heublein, the first American manufacturer of vodka. This cocktail was invented in America, but the name comes from the capital of the land of vodka and the powerful, mule-like kick of the ginger flavor.

The original recipe calls for ginger beer, which has a very powerful aroma and ginger taste, but since it's difficult to get in Japan, ginger ale is typically used instead. Ginger ale comes in many brands with different flavors. I like Wilkinson, which has a relatively strong kick and ginger bouquet. The proportion of vodka to ginger ale should be 1:1 or 1:1.5. Use more than this and you'll lose that unique kick which defines the Moscow Mule.

The standard recipe calls for lime juice, but I use fresh limes. Again, some people use half-cut limes, but I prefer quarter-cut limes that are visible from above the mug. You have to be careful with limes because some have very thick skins and little juice. When this is the case, I add fresh lime juice that I have squeezed separately.

Optimally, the mug is a two-wall copper mug, since this is easiest to drink from and the outside doesn't get covered in condensation. This two-wall construction might not be the best to communicate that deep-chilled feeling, however. If I serve a Moscow Mule in a tumbler I use half-cut limes and include a muddler, à la a Gin Rickey.

Standard Recipe
1 1/2 ounce vodka
1/2 ounce lime juice
Ginger beer

Uyeda Recipe
1 1/2 ounce vodka (Smirnoff)
Fresh lime juice of 1/4 lime
Ginger ale (Wilkinson)

Glass: copper mug (chilled in freezer)

Add vodka to a copper mug filled with crushed ice and squeeze in a quarter-cut lime, then dropping it into the mug. Fill with ginger ale.

SEA BREEZE

シー・ブリーズ

This is an American cocktail that was introduced to Japan around 1980. Although it's a summer cocktail, it doesn't evoke a hot summer sun for me as much as it does a gentle breeze on the beach. It's one of my favorite standard cocktails. It has a light feel and can be enjoyed like a soft drink.

The Sea Breeze uses cranberry juice, a relatively new ingredient, and has a drier lightness, which is popular. This drink can be built, but the usual method now in Japan is to shake and then pour it over ice.

Cranberry juice has a strong tart component and not too much sweetness, which makes it ideal for use in cocktails that don't use a lot of sugar. It's good for making original cocktails as well.

A trend among guests in recent years has been towards less sweet cocktails, particularly among women. For this reason, the Sea Breeze, with its restrained sweetness and low alcohol level, is a particular favorite with women. Toning down the hue of the color is a good match for the name, I think.

Another plus of a Sea Breeze is that you can adjust the amount of alcohol to match a guest's preference by using more or less vodka (but being careful not to disrupt the balance).

I serve guests who can't drink any alcohol a Virgin Breeze, which is a variation of the Sea Breeze. I shake fresh grapefruit juice and cranberry juice in a 2:1 ratio and serve on ice.

Standard Recipe
1 part vodka
1 part cranberry juice
1 part grapefruit juice

Uyeda Recipe
1 part vodka (Smirnoff)
1 part cranberry juice (Del Monte)
1 part fresh grapefruit juice

Glass: rocks glass

Shake the vodka, cranberry juice, and fresh grapefruit juice in a shaker. Serve on ice in a rocks glass.

RUM-BASE STANDARD COCKTAILS

DAIQUIRI ダイキリ

3:1 – this is indisputably the best balance between a base spirit and a sour ingredient. The sourness is present but not overpowered, which is why I consider the Daiquiri the foundation of its own category of short drink.

The Daiquiri was named for an iron mine in the south of Cuba. It's said that this cocktail got its start when workers toiling in the fierce heat mixed Cuba's unique rum with lime and sugar. Perhaps the combination of lime juice and sugar refreshed their weary bones.

When mixing a Daiquiri, stick to the recipe. It's not an exaggeration to say that this is the only way to make a good Daiquiri. Never disrupt the 3:1 balance of the alcohol to the sour component.

One thing I insist on using is fresh lime juice. Some recipes use lemons, but that's a different drink. If you consider the history behind the Daiquiri, then you'll understand the importance of maintaining both the sweetness and the sourness.

The main ingredient is white rum, which doesn't vary very much in strength among brands, meaning no particular brand is better or worse for using the hard shake, so use whichever brand you prefer. Incidentally, I use Lemon Hart.

I use a triangular cocktail glass to represent the three elements: the iron mine, the sourness and the refreshing flavor.

Standard Recipe	Uyeda Recipe
3 parts white rum	3 parts white rum (Lemon Hart)
1 part lime juice	1 part fresh lime juice
1 teaspoon sugar	1 teaspoon sugar syrup

Glass: cocktail glass

Shake the white rum, fresh lime juice and sugar syrup in a shaker. Serve in a cocktail glass.

BACARDI

The Bacardi Company, as part of a marketing campaign, created this cocktail after the lifting of Prohibition in 1933, and the original recipe called for using Bacardi white rum. At one point, the State Supreme Court of New York even ordered bars that were serving Bacardis using rum made by other companies to use Bacardi rum.

RUM-BASE STANDARD COCKTAILS

A Bacardi is basically a Daiquiri with the addition of grenadine, creating the pink color characteristic of this cocktail. Grenadine is used to add both the color and the sweetness, but if it's used as the only sweet ingredient, the color will be too dark. Use only as much grenadine as you need to reproduce the desired color, and use sugar syrup to compensate for the sweetness. This is important.

There are some who call Bacardis *Daiquiris*, saying that the pink color was the color of the sun setting behind the Daiquiri iron mine, but generally around the world Daiquiris are white and Bacardis are pink.

Because of their history, Daiquiris are best served in glasses with sharp lines, but a Bacardi is best served in a curved glass, which better suits the soft color.

Standard Recipe

3 parts Bacardi white rum
1 part lime juice
1 teaspoon grenadine

Uyeda Recipe

3 parts Bacardi white rum
1 part fresh lime juice
1 teaspoon grenadine (Meijiya)
1 teaspoon sugar syrup

Glass: cocktail glass

Shake the Bacardi rum, fresh lime juice, grenadine syrup and sugar syrup in a shaker. Serve in a cocktail glass.

FROZEN DAIQUIRI フローズン・ダイキリ

This drink was created in Havana and is notorious for being a favorite of Hemingway's. The drink conjures an image of Hemingway sitting on a beach somewhere under the hot sun drinking this bone-chillingly cold cocktail.

The standard style is a lot more liquid than the smooth sherbet that I make. The kind of Frozen Daiquiri that Hemingway drank was this liquid type. If you reduce the amount of ice used, you'll achieve this liquid consistency, but unfortunately it can seem watery. That's why I use a bit more ice to create the sherbet consistency. It's a cocktail that you can almost eat.

On the other hand, if you use too much ice, you'll lose the flavor, but you can avoid this by starting off with a small amount of ice in the blender and then adding more as you blend it, until it reaches the right consistency.

As a rule, I use Cointreau, which is a white curaçao, instead of maraschino. Cointreau adds a fullness that simple syrup alone cannot achieve. Garnishing with a mint leaf adds to the freshness of the drink.

The Frozen Daiquiri could be considered the origin of all frozen-style cocktails, so it comes in many variations. Some people use maraschino, and some people even put lime peel into the blender.

One very popular Frozen Daiquiri uses actual fruit such as strawberries, peaches, or bananas, which have a smooth liquid consistency. On the other hand, if you use lemon, you can't get that smoothness, so I add some meringue egg whites to compensate.

Standard Recipe
1 1/2 ounce white rum
1 teaspoon maraschino
1/2 ounce lime juice
1 teaspoon sugar
Crushed ice

Uyeda Recipe
1½ ounce white rum (Lemon Hart)
1 teaspoon Cointreau
1/2 ounce fresh lime juice
1 teaspoon sugar syrup
1 cup crushed ice
Mint leaf

Glass: champagne saucer or cocktail glass

Blend the white rum, Cointreau (white curaçao), fresh lime juice, sugar syrup and crushed ice in a blender. Serve in a champagne saucer with a spoon and a straw. Garnish with a mint leaf.

TEQUILA-BASE STANDARD COCKTAILS

MARGARITA   マルガリータ

This cocktail was invented in 1949 as an entry in a Los Angeles cocktail competition. The entrant named it after his girlfriend, who was felled by a stray hunting bullet in her youth. This romantic story helped create the popularity of this drink, and today it can be found all over the world. Of all the cocktails we've seen so far with encrusted rims, most have used sugar, but a Margarita uses salt. Perhaps this salt is supposed to represent the young man's sorrow.

The original recipe called for 1$^{1}/_{2}$ ounce of tequila, 1 ounce of lime juice, 1 ounce of lemon juice and $^{1}/_{4}$ ounce of white curaçao. As you can see by looking at the recipe, this is a Daiquiri-type cocktail that is very sour. The Margarita used to be made with ice crushed in a blender, making it halfway between a frozen cocktail and a shaken cocktail.

As the Margarita spread throughout the world, it was refined and eventually it became a Sidecar-type recipe with less sourness. The mixing method was also simplified to simple shaking. Today I use the original Daiquiri-type recipe for guests who prefer a sour taste.

As I've said before, whenever a recipe calls for lime juice, I use fresh limes. Furthermore, in order to present the salt-encrusted rims beautifully, you shouldn't chill the glass. Use a glass that is room temperature, and do not fill the glass to the top. One popular variation is a Frozen Margarita. Frozen cocktails are typically served with a straw, but since the salt is an important component of the flavor in a Margarita, no straw is provided.

Standard Recipe
2 parts tequila
1 part white curaçao
1 part lime juice

Uyeda Recipe
4 parts tequila (Sauza)
1 part Cointreau
1 part fresh lemon juice

Glass: cocktail glass (room temperature)
Shake the tequila, Cointreau (white curaçao) and fresh lime juice in a shaker. Serve in a cocktail glass with a salt-encrusted rim.

LIQUEUR-BASE STANDARD COCKTAILS

GRASSHOPPER グラスホッパー

This is good example of a cocktail that uses fresh cream and is a perfect candidate for a hard shake, which is suited to mixing the hard-to-mix fresh cream and liqueurs. It's important to shake the ingredients long enough so that condensation forms on the outside of the shaker. By doing this, you'll achieve a whipped, creamy consistency.

The grasshopper is a good cocktail to make when you're practicing a hard shake. It froths easily because you're mixing a sweet liqueur into fresh cream. If the result has a thick consistency, then you've mastered the hard shake. If you overdo it, however, it becomes watery, so be careful.

The standard recipe calls for equal amounts of three ingredients, but to reduce the sweetness a bit I upped the amount of crème de cacao and reduced the amount of crème de menthe and fresh cream.

The grasshopper is named for the color of the drink, and for this reason I use white crème de cacao, even though dark crème de cacao tastes better. If your preference is for flavor, you can mix equal amounts of white and dark crème de cacao. Avoid using only dark crème de cacao, though, because the resulting cocktail will look more like something that ought to be called a cicada than a grasshopper.

Standard Recipe
- 1 part white crème de cacao
- 1 part green crème de menthe
- 1 part fresh cream

Uyeda Recipe
- 2 parts white crème de cacao (Bols)
- 1 part crème de menthe (Get 27)
- 1 part fresh cream

Glass: cocktail glass

Shake the crème de cacao, crème de menthe and fresh cream in a shaker. Serve in a cocktail glass.

VALENCIA

The Valencia is named after Spain's famous orange-growing region. The apricot brandy and orange juice combination manages to avoid a cloying sweetness, instead providing a particularly pleasing aromatic orange lightness that is quite seductive.

This combination can easily be varied: by reversing the proportions, adding grenadine, etc. That said, if you want to serve a drink and call it a Valencia, then the limit is 1:1 for the basic ingredients.

The apricot brandy I use is Lejay's Crème d'Abricots for its unrivaled color and aroma. Oranges greatly vary in taste depending on the season as well as where they were grown, so adjust accordingly. If the oranges you're using lack sweetness, then up the apricot brandy a bit. If they're very sweet, pull back on the brandy. You can also make adjustments according to how strong the guest wants the drink.

Remember, you'll mostly find navel oranges in winter (these have a shiny peel and are dimpled at the top), but these don't have a lot of juice; so, as the name of the drink indicates, use Valencia oranges if you can.

A word about bitters: unfortunately, it's almost impossible anymore to find bitters that are actually bitter. And if you can't find decent bitters, it's better not to add them at all. The flavor is cleaner and better balanced that way.

Standard Recipe	Uyeda Recipe
2 parts apricot brandy	2 parts crème d'abricots (Lejay)
1 part orange juice	1 part fresh orange juice
4 dashes orange bitters	

Glass: cocktail glass

Shake the crème d'abricots (apricot brandy) and fresh orange juice in a shaker. Serve in a cocktail glass.

CHARLIE CHAPLIN チャーリー・チャップリン

One of a relatively new style of cocktail that involves shaking the ingredients and then serving on ice. The advantage of this method is the ability to keep a shaken cocktail cool. The downside is the risk of watering the cocktail down because of the ice. The best way to prevent this is to make sure the ingredients are shaken correctly. You want a sharp, clean flavor.

Crème d'abricots is a type of apricot brandy, and Lejay's has a particularly good color and aroma, which is why I use it. Sloe gin is a liqueur made from sloe berries, which belong to the same family as plums and apricots. It's a dark crimson color. Sloe gin started out as a dry flavored gin but has morphed into a very sweet liqueur, which is rather unfortunate.

It also used to have a lower specific gravity, and I would use it in one of my original cocktails called a Kyonishiki, but since it's become heavier I can no longer make the Kyonishiki, now forgotten in the mists of time.

This recipe doesn't actually show the very fine adjustment to the proportions I use. I use just a dash more sloe gin than crème d'abricots. Despite being a liqueur-base cocktail, the shaken/on-the-rocks style allows the fresh lightness of the ingredients to come through.

Standard Recipe
- 1 part sloe gin
- 1 part apricot brandy
- 1 part lemon juice

Uyeda Recipe
- 1 part sloe gin (Bols)
- 1 part crème d'abricots (Lejay)
- 1 part fresh lemon juice

Glass: rocks glass

Shake the sloe gin (sloe berry liqueur), crème d'abricots (apricot brandy) and fresh lemon juice in a shaker and serve on ice.

WINE-BASE STANDARD COCKTAILS

BELLINI

This cocktail was created around 1948 by Giuseppe Cipriani, the owner of the famous Harry's Bar in Venice, Italy, in honor of an exhibition of works by Giovanni Bellini. It has only recently become popular in Japan. Considering this background, it would be logical to use spumante, the

Italian sparkling wine, but I prefer to take the grade up one notch and use champagne, which has a more nuanced flavor.

The Bellini has a subtle peach flavor that expands with the bubbles, making this one of the most popular drinks in my bar. Blending canned white peaches, peach liqueur and grenadine in a blender makes the peach nectar that defines the flavor of the Bellini. The grenadine that is added to the nectar is not included in the recipe of the cocktail. Make certain you don't use too much, otherwise it will overpower the flavor of the white peach. I make a large batch of the nectar and keep it for use in other original cocktails.

In order to protect the fine carbonation of the champagne, I pour the champagne into the glass first. The peach nectar follows, slowly and gently. Then slowly stir the ingredients.

It goes without saying that the champagne and the peach nectar should be chilled. If you can do all this correctly, you might be able to top the great Bellini they serve at Harry's Bar.

Standard Recipe

2 parts sparkling wine
1 part peach nectar
1 dash grenadine syrup

Uyeda Recipe

3 parts brut champagne
1 part peach nectar (homemade)

Glass: fluted champagne glass

Pour the champagne into a champagne glass, followed by the peach nectar, pouring slowly. Stir only a few times.

BAMBOO

バンブー

This drink has a sharp finish and is an ideal apéritif. To achieve a clearer flavor, I add the fresh aroma of a lemon peel and skip the orange bitters. This cocktail is supposed to evoke a Japanese feel (hence the name). It switches the sweet vermouth of an Adonis with dry vermouth. The chief bartender at Yokohama's Grand Hotel, Louis Eppinger, invented the

Bamboo. He made it for foreigners visiting Japan, and it was through these visitors that its fame spread around the world.

The importance of skillful stirring cannot be overstated with this cocktail. It must be well mixed and well chilled. The simplicity of the ingredients makes a good stir all the more important.

I recommend serving a Bamboo in a slim glass with sharp lines to match the pale color of the chilled drink. If a guest wants a drier Bamboo, the limit is 5:1 with the dry vermouth.

An original variation on the Adonis and Bamboo is the Petit Prélude, which uses rosé vermouth. The dry sherry and rosé vermouth are stirred in a 3:1 ratio. The gentle botanical aroma and refined wine bouquet of the rosé vermouth create a gentle flavor, so I suggest leaving off the lemon peel for the Petit Prélude.

Standard Recipe	*Uyeda Recipe*
2 parts dry sherry	3 parts dry sherry (Tio Pepe)
1 part dry vermouth	1 part dry vermouth (Noilly Prat)
1 dash orange bitters	Lemon peel

Glass: cocktail glass

Stir the dry sherry and dry vermouth in a mixing glass and serve in a cocktail glass. Garnish with a lemon peel.

KIR ROYAL

キール・ロワイヤル

The Kir Royal replaces the extremely dry white wine of a Kir with champagne. This is one of the most famous champagne cocktails and is popular as an apéritif.

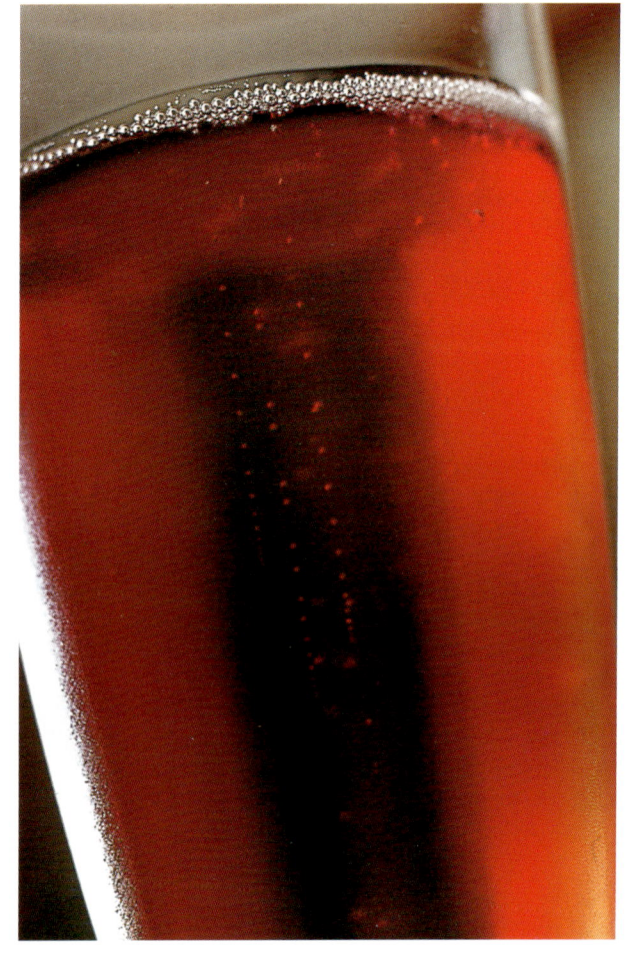

As in a Kir, I use very dry champagne for the base and reduce the amount of cassis to match Japanese taste. Just the right amount of sweetness stimulates the appetite, which is what an apéritif should do. Since no ice is used, the champagne and the glass should be chilled ahead of time.

Sparkling wines from all over the world have become available at reasonable prices in recent years, and there's no reason you couldn't use a less expensive sparking wine in this drink. However, it is a Kir Royal, after all, so I think it's better to use champagne from the Champagne region of France to achieve the proper nobility of flavor and bouquet.

You should finish a champagne bottle the day it's opened, but with a special cork, it can hold for two days. I use the crème de cassis made by Lejay, because it has a reliably consistent color and flavor, something a lot of other brands lack.

This is a built cocktail, and the crème de cassis goes in first, followed by the champagne ~ both poured ever so gently to avoid flattening the carbonation. The two ingredients mix well this way. Avoid metal barspoons for this drink, since champagne does not react well to metal.

There are many other cocktails that use champagne ~ champagne with orange juice is a Mimosa; with dark beer, a Black Velvet; with peach nectar, a Bellini; with black sambuca, a Black Rain; and with crème de framboise, a Kir Imperial. Almost all of them are enjoyed as apéritifs.

Standard Recipe	Uyeda Recipe
4 parts champagne	9 parts brut champagne
1 part crème de cassis	1 part crème de cassis (Lejay)

Glass: fluted champagne glass

Pour the crème de cassis into a champagne glass and then add the champagne in several small pours. Turn once with a barspoon to aid the natural mixing of the ingredients.

CATEGORIES OF SHAKEN COCKTAILS

	SIDECAR TYPE 4:1:1	**DAIQUIRI TYPE 3:1**
DESCRIPTION	These are cocktails that have a ratio of base liquor to sweet ingredient to sour ingredient of 2:1:1 in the standard recipe, the sweet component and the sour component balancing each other out. I use a drier 4:1:1 ratio.	These cocktails have a ratio of 3:1 of the base liquor to a sour ingredient, making them sourer. I use sugar syrup as a sweetener.
EXAMPLES	White Lady Sidecar Margarita Balalaika XYZ Olympic Champs Élysées Paradise Flamingo Blue Moon Kamikaze Mockingbird	Gimlet Jack Rose New York Daiquiri Bacardi Sledgehammer

ORIGINAL COCKTAILS

How Colors Add to Flavor

The City Coral is a coral-style cocktail that evokes a coral reef by means of the sugar-encrusted rim around the glass, which gives off a cool aquamarine glow. The bright blue-green color deepens the impression of a calm sea. In this section I'll talk about how to create colors that heighten the effect and appeal of a cocktail.

As I've said before, cocktails are drinks that are made by combining a number of different ingredients, many of which come in very bright colors—especially liqueurs. Obviously mixed cocktails will take on these colors, and this is one way that the image of a cocktail is created. In some cases combining a number of different ingredients can result in unexpectedly bright and beautiful colorings.

One example is the combination of blue curaçao (Bols) with whiskey. This is the key to the combination of ingredients in my original King's Valley cocktail, which has a color I discovered by trying various ingredients with blue curaçao. It's also one example of the ability to create green without using a green ingredient.

Other examples include striking colors such as the yellow created by combining melon liqueur (which is green) and apricot brandy (which is orange) as in the Kalos Kyma; and the pale pastel blue created by combining blue curaçao (blue) and grapefruit juice. Red is the one color that has been impossible to reproduce.

A small amount of liqueur can sometimes be added to boost a color, particularly when a color has been diffused by the combination of many different ingredients. For example, a blue ingredient is effective to deepen a green and a red ingredient is effective to deepen a blue.

Color and decoration are important elements in creating cocktails. However, a cocktail has to be eye-catching and not just strange, and the cocktail has to be something that guests will like and want to have again.

In this sense, a complete familiarity with the standard repertoire of cocktails that is at the foundation of cocktail mixing is essential if you want to create your own original cocktails.

BLUE + YELLOW = GREEN

Combining blue curaçao (left) and yellow whiskey (middle) results in the intermediate green King's Valley (right).

ORANGE + GREEN = YELLOW

Combining orange apricot brandy (left) and green melon liqueur (middle) results in the intermediate yellow $K\alpha\lambda o\varsigma\ K\upsilon\mu\alpha$ (right).

GREEN + GRAPEFRUIT JUICE = YELLOW GREEN
YELLOW GREEN + BLUE = GREEN

Adding a bit of blue curaçao to a green ingredient such as a melon liqueur has the effect of deepening the green. In a City Coral, green melon liqueur (left) is combined with grapefruit juice (second from left), which results in a pale yellow color (middle). Adding blue curaçao to this (second from right) has the effect of restoring the original bright green color (right).

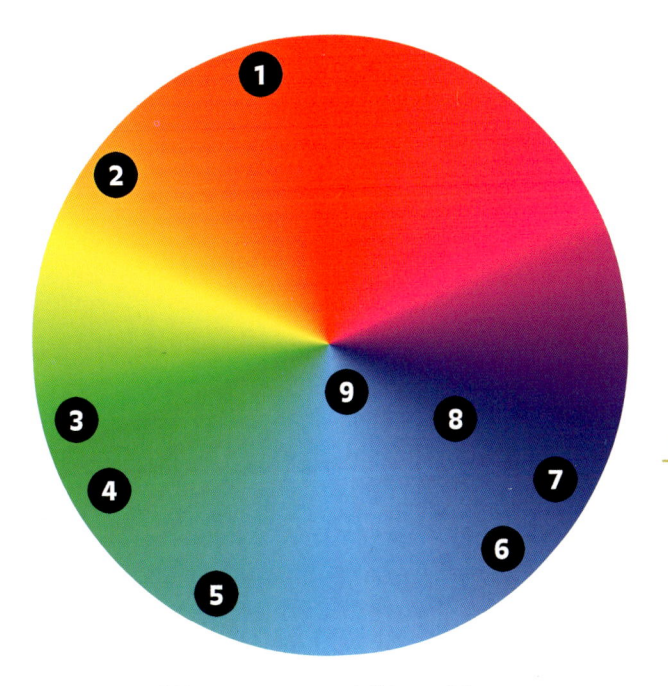

1. Left Alone
2. Καλος Κυμα
3. King's Valley
4. Hong Kong Connection
5. Blue Trip
6. Fisherman & Son
7. Aquamarine
8. Fantastic Léman
9. M-30 Rain

137

PRIZE WINNERS

PURE LOVE　　　　　　　　　　　　　　ピュア・ラブ

MY FIRST PRIZE WINNER

In 1979, when I had just joined the All Nippon Bartenders Association, I went to a national competition held at the Palace Hotel and saw my first bartending competition. The atmosphere was electric as I watched the bartenders display their skills on stage ~ it was an amazing experience, which impelled me to enter a competition myself. I wanted to test my experience of 15 years and the fruits of my labor against other competitors.

As luck would have it, 1979 was the year Suntory came out with their Tropical Cocktail drink, which marked Suntory's serious entry into the cocktail market. I had the sense that a cocktail boom would start in four or five years, and it seemed like a good time for me to try my hand at competition. I was extremely excited.

Still, I would be turning 36 years old the next year, which I thought was too old to be entering a competition for the first time. Almost all the first-time competitors were in their 20s, and when I looked at them, I felt like an old timer among children. What if I lost to one of these whippersnappers? I felt a lot of pressure, but when I look back I realize how lucky I was to be able to enter a national competition the year after entering the association.

Strictly speaking, this was the second cocktail I had ever submitted to a competition. The first, in April 1980, was a cocktail I called a Papito created for the First Suntory Tropical Cocktail Contest after I had been accepted to compete in the national competition. I wanted to have the experience of being in competition and mixing cocktails in front of people in that kind of atmosphere.

My second competitive creation was the Pure Love, which was based on a Gin Fizz. In the early days of Japanese cocktails gin-based cocktails were the norm, and the Gin Fizz was the most popular.

The basic method for making a long drink was to make a short drink and add soda or some other kind of carbonated ingredient. In keeping with this, I decided to use gin as the base. Next came the sour and sweet ingredients. I decided to use fresh lime juice, which was still relatively unknown at that time, instead of lemon juice, and raspberry liqueur, also only rarely imported at the time, instead of sugar syrup. Novelty is an important element in competition judging.

Next I had to decide what carbonated ingredient to use. I tried using soda first, but it overpowered the base cocktail. Next I tried tonic water, to try and make up for some of the lost volume with sweetness, but this took away from the freshness of the flavor. Finally, I thought of ginger ale, and it was a perfect match. I decided to use this cocktail in the competition.

To name the cocktail I took the word pure from a Shiseido campaign slogan (My *Pure Lady*) that they were using when I worked there (at Bar l'Osier, a restaurant run by the company) and the word *love* to match the bittersweet flavor of the cocktail.

With this newly created Pure Love in hand, I went to Hiroshima, where the competition was to be held. I was girded with enthusiasm and not much else, since I didn't even know what to do to train ahead of time. The one thing that I couldn't decide on until the last minute was the timing for placing the ice in the glass.

During the competition you had to mix your cocktail in one five-serving batch. Past competitors had told me that if you put the ice in the glass ahead of time, you could cover if you messed up and poured different amounts into each of the five glasses. So, that's what most people did.

All five glasses had to be poured to the same level, and I thought it would be better if I could show the judges that I could do it accurately. Plus, if you considered the temperature of the competition hall, placing the ice in the glasses ahead of time would cause it to melt, resulting in a watery cocktail. That was my case for putting the ice in a glass afterwards. I spent a sleepless night in my hotel room before the competition trying to figure out whether to put the ice in first or last.

It rained the day of the competition. I was going on second. People who go on first tend to receive lower scores, but I think it was good that I went on without having seen many people compete first.

In the end I decided to pour the shaken cocktail into the five tumblers lined up on the counter first and then put in the ice. If the levels were wrong in the glasses, that would be that, of course, so all I could do was have faith in my ability.

The levels of glasses matched perfectly. I had done it! In the heat of competition you don't have time to think about winning or losing, but I was at least satisfied that I had done what I needed to. And the judges agreed. I got first place, probably for the novelty of the ingredients I had selected and for the fact that I had put the ice in last.

As soon as the tension and nerves from the competition were gone, I was stricken with a horrible stomach cramp, and stomach medicine has been my constant companion in competitions since then.

Following my first ever win, I was honored by being appointed director of the ANBA. It was a fantastic start to my competition career. Thanks to all that hard work, the Pure Love, my first original cocktail, is still the most special to me. Just like a first love.

1 ounce dry gin (Gordon's)
1/2 ounce crème de framboise (Gabriel)
1/2 ounce fresh lime juice
Ginger ale (Canada Dry)

Glass: tumbler

Shake the dry gin, crème de framboise and fresh lime juice in a shaker. Pour into a tumbler, put in two or three pieces of cracked ice and fill with ginger ale. Garnish with a slice of lime.

Note: This cocktail won first place in the Long Drink category at the 1980 All Nippon Bartenders Association Cocktail Competition, the first time a debut competitor ever received this honor.

FANTASTIC LÉMAN

This is the first cocktail that I ever submitted to an international competition. The competition was held in Geneva, Switzerland. When I saw the list of approved ingredients, I was surprised to see Japanese sake on it, since it was still a relatively rare ingredient in those days. I chose it without hesitating. The only problem with Japanese sake is that its flavor lacks impact. I gave a lot of thought to what ingredients could be combined with it, and after consulting with Kiyoshi Imai who worked at the Palace Hotel back then, I decided to try to create a cocktail that would embody Lake Geneva (Lac Léman to the French).

Having already decided to incorporate Japanese sake, I then chose Cointreau, which is a clear liquor that would serve to act as the center of the flavor. To this I added Detling kirschwasser, a specialty of Switzerland. In this way I hoped to bring Japan and Switzerland together in one cocktail. People often *pay homage* to the host country in this manner in international competitions. Next I chose fresh lemon juice as the sour ingredient. In order to fill out the volume of the flavor, I picked tonic water instead of soda. I wanted to use clear ingredients and then add blue curaçao in a layered gradation, so as to express the depth and transparency of the lake.

Although I was using Japanese sake, I didn't want its flavor to be too present in front. Instead I wanted to define the flavor using the Cointreau and lemon juice to enclose the sake, as it were.

When I arrived in Switzerland, I looked down over Lake Geneva from the mountains of Lausanne and was gratified to see that the color of the lake and the color of the cocktail were exactly alike. I'll never forget that moment.

Unfortunately, all that was available on the day the competition was a purple-hued blue curaçao. I had brought the sake with me but didn't imagine in a million years that I would get tripped up by the blue curaçao. I protested to no avail. There was nothing to do but use the purple blue curaçao. Obviously I wasn't able to achieve the blue of the lake, which had to remain a dream.

- 5 parts Japanese sake
- 3 parts Cointreau
- 1 part kirsch liqueur (Bols)
- 1 part fresh lemon juice
- 1 teaspoon blue curaçao (Bols)
- Tonic water

Glass: Collins glass

Shake the Japanese sake (rice liquor), Cointreau (white curaçao), kirsch liqueur and fresh lemon juice in a shaker. Pour into a Collins glass filled with ice. Add the tonic water and then layer the blue curaçao, creating layers of colors. Serve with a muddler in the glass.

Note: This cocktail represented Japan in the World Cocktail Festival organized by the International Bartenders Association in 1981. It received the silver medal.

TOKIO

I started creating a cocktail for the next international competition, which was going to be held in Germany following year. The theme was *apéritifs*. The image of an apéritif in Japan at that time was of a drink with very sharp flavors. However, looking back over the data for previous international competitions, I noticed that winning cocktails had generally been on the sweet side, almost all of them using some kind of liqueur. Compared to the general trend in cocktails, there was a large discrepancy in terms of the sweetness of apéritifs between Japan on one hand and, on the other hand, Europe and the United States, where sweetness was preferred.

PRIZE WINNERS

I figured the only thing to do was to make a cocktail using a medium-sweet liqueur. Vermouth was known as an apéritif, so I chose rosé vermouth, which was fairly new at that time. As a sign of respect for the host country, I chose a German liqueur called pampelmuse. Since this would be a cocktail based on a liqueur, I used vodka to bolster the base, which resulted in a slightly sweet apéritif with a soft character.

I picked the name *Tokio* because this cocktail would be representing Japan in the competition.

Back then, all I could think about was winning the international competition, and I was very confident that if I could win the German competition, which was essentially an elimination round for the international competition, I would win the international competition, too.

Arrogance is a frightening thing. It had laid a trap of unbelievable proportions. During training, I had used room temperature vodka, but on the day of the competition I accidentally used vodka which had been chilled in a refrigerator. Because the vodka was cold, the ice didn't melt as I had expected, and this threw off the proportions of the ingredients.

Naturally, I didn't win, and the reason I didn't think ahead and didn't stay on my toes was that I had become very arrogant. Today I almost feel a sense of penitence towards this cocktail because of this. It's one of my favorite cocktails, and I often serve it as a long drink with soda.

> 3 parts vodka (Smirnoff)
> 2 parts rosé vermouth (Martini)
> 1 part pampelmuse (Specht)
> 1 teaspoon fresh lime juice
> 1 maraschino cherry

Glass: cocktail glass

Shake the vodka, vermouth and pampelmuse (grapefruit liqueur) in a shaker. Serve in a cocktail glass. Include a maraschino cherry on a cocktail spear.

Note: This cocktail won second place in the skills category at the 1983 All Nippon Bartenders Association Cocktail Competition.

CITY CORAL

The most noticeable feature of this cocktail is probably the coral frosting on the outside of the glass. Decorating the rim of the glass with colorful liqueurs instead of fruit juice is a style that has been around for a long time, and this is an extension of that. The first cocktail to popularize this style was the City Coral.

Using this style was a large part of my original intent in creating this cocktail. There is a broad spectrum of colors to choose from, depending on the liqueur you use, but blue curaçao and grenadine (which is red) were two colors that did not lose their intensity when combined with salt, so I limited myself to these two ingredients. I combined this style with various cocktails, and found that blue was the best match.

I also wanted to make a cocktail that would have broad popularity and decided to use Midori, a melon liqueur made by Suntory, which, after a considerable hiatus, was again being imported into Japan from the US.

It was not long before I settled on a combination of gin and fresh grapefruit juice. I picked grapefruit juice because it goes well with salt (cf., a Salty Dog). Lastly, I added tonic water to fill out the flavor a bit.

I still wasn't completely satisfied with the color, however. The taste was fine, but the yellow-green color looked a bit faded. To achieve a deeper and more colorful green, I added a teaspoon of Bols blue curaçao.

Thanks to the combination of the coral style, the bright green color and the accessible flavor as well as the heart and soul that poured into this drink, the City Coral won first place in a national competition, gaining the highest score ever awarded to a cocktail.

It wasn't so successful in international competitions, where cocktails with salt-encrusted rims aren't rated so highly because the tongue comes directly in contact with the salt. Other bartenders at the competition were fascinated by the coral frosting, however, and asked me many questions about it.

> 2/3 ounce dry gin (Beefeater)
> 2/3 ounce melon liqueur (Midori)
> 2/3 ounce fresh grapefruit juice
> 1 teaspoon blue curaçao (Bols)
> Tonic water

Glass: *coral glass (room temperature)*

Use salt and blue curaçao to create the coral frosting around the glass. Mix the dry gin, melon liqueur, fresh grapefruit juice and blue curaçao in a shaker. Pour into the glass, insert cracked ice and fill with tonic water.

Note: This cocktail won first place at the All Nippon Bartenders Association Cocktail Competition National Round, which was also a preliminary round for the 1984 International Cocktail Competition held by the International Bartenders Association, where the cocktail represented Japan.

KING'S VALLEY

This cocktail's biggest selling point is undoubtedly its color. In fact, the King's Valley cocktail marks the first time a bright green color was created without using any green ingredients. Perhaps it was because of this that I started being called the color magician. (See the section on color combinations.)

Two years previously, in 1984, I had been using different liqueurs to try to find a way to deepen the color of blue curaçao to a kind of ink blue for the Misty cocktail which I was working on, and I accidentally came across this color. The combination of whiskey and blue curaçao, which might have remained hidden in a corner of my brain if I hadn't been working on a submission for a scotch competition, finally saw the light of day.

Since the color is the defining characteristic of this cocktail, I decided to make it a short drink with a tight flavor, instead of diluting it as a long drink. I looked through the documentation for the competition and didn't find any Sidecar-type cocktails that combined Cointreau and lemon juice with a whiskey base, so I decided to go with that. The proportions match my basic pattern for a short (Sidecar-type) drink of 4:1:1. I replaced the lemon juice with fresh lime juice in keeping with the current trends. This was key in creating a light finish, which was a good contrast with the sweet image created by the color.

The name is a combination of the king of liquors, scotch, with the valleys where it is made. Thus, this king of the green valley was born. I wanted the green to be a cloudy color that brought to mind the moors of Scotland without being too blue or too pastel colored.

The scotch I originally used was Grant's, but today I use Whyte & McKay or Old Parr. Shaking scotch brings out a particular kind of bitterness, but Whyte & McKay is a decidedly sensitive whiskey that doesn't suffer from this bitterness even if shaken.

Just recently a guest requested I make it using Old Parr, and I found that the whiskey flavor remains solidly in the foreground without any annoying bitterness.

4 parts scotch (originally Grant's)
1 part Cointreau
1 part fresh lime juice
1 teaspoon blue curaçao (Bols)

Glass: cocktail glass

Shake the scotch, Cointreau (white curaçao), fresh lime juice and blue curaçao in a shaker. Serve in a cocktail glass.

Note: This cocktail won first place in the 1st Scotch Whiskey Cocktail Contest held by the Scotch Whiskey Press Center and three other groups in 1986. The only rule in this competition is that scotch must be used.

JEALOUSY

The first *Artist of Artists* New Cocktail Contest was held by the Cocktail Communication Society in Tokyo in November, 1996. This competition features ten bartenders who are picked ahead of time, and the grand prize is decided by tasting by the 250 members of the CCS and by visitors.

The first theme was *cocktails for women*. To me this meant that the cocktail created had to be sweet and colorful ~ I imagined the majority of the cocktails would be red or pink in pastel hues. They would also be given a name evoking images of feminine softness and beauty.

PRIZE WINNERS

I decided to swim against this current by calling my cocktail something racier: Jealousy. I also went with the color yellow. I used a yellow liqueur called mirabelle that has a well-mannered personality and which mixes well with other ingredients.

I chose vodka as the base spirit, an orange liqueur called Bols Premier for the sweetness and fresh grapefruit juice for the sourness since it has a kind of feminine softness and lightness. All the ingredients blended together very easily.

It was after this that I ran into trouble. I tried using the basic 4:1:1 ratio for short drinks, but the result was kind of watery. I tried changing the proportions in different ways and finally settled on reducing the amount of vodka, for a 2:1:1 ratio of vodka, Premier and grapefruit juice.

Black matches yellow, and I wanted to use something black to garnish the drink, which I achieved with a black olive. In order to emphasize this contrast on the day of the competition, I brought my own cocktail glass to the venue. It had a sharp, slim form and was triangular.

This cocktail has a clean flavor with limited sweetness. It has a sharp, modern image mixing yellow and black. It also has an eye-catching name. These elements came together and helped me win a grand prize. One of the female judges praised my cocktail saying, "Women are not all sweetness and light. This cocktail befits a modern woman."

2 parts vodka (Smirnoff)
1 part Premier (Bols)
1 part fresh grapefruit juice
1 teaspoon mirabelle (Oldesloer)

Glass: cocktail glass

Shake the vodka, Premier (orange curaçao), grapefruit juice and mirabelle (yellow plum liqueur) in a shaker. Serve in a cocktail glass.

Note: This cocktail won the Grand Prix at the first *Artist of Artists* New Cocktail Contest held by the Cocktail Communication Society in Tokyo in 1996. The theme of the contest was *cocktails for women*.

LEFT ALONE

The next year's competition had a *cocktails for men* theme. For this I was going to make a dry cocktail with a slightly softer finish. Still, I picked an edgier name this time, too, taking the title of a jazz standard – *Left Alone*. I liked the song, but more than that I wanted to evoke the lonely image of a man whose woman has left him.

Bourbon was the natural choice for a base. It perfectly fit the image of a man who's been left. The question was how dry to make it.

As always, I started with a ratio of 4:1:1. I chose Premier as the sweet component and fresh grapefruit as the sour component because I thought that a too-sour ingredient would stifle the flavor of the bourbon. Unfortunately, the grapefruit was a bit too watery, so I switched to lime juice for a cleaner finish.

I wanted a unique look and aimed for a sepia color by adding one teaspoon of martini bitters. No garnish, either. The image had to be stark.

Unfortunately, I didn't get first prize. The lime juice was probably a bit too sour and the character of the bourbon overpowered the other ingredients. Another problem may have been the name. The competition was supposed to be festive, and the name *Left Alone* was probably a bit too dark for the expectations of the judges. Changing the proportions to 2 parts bourbon, 1 part Premier, 1 part Martini bitters and 1 tablespoon of fresh lime juice makes the flavor a bit more accessible.

4 parts bourbon (Wild Turkey 8 Year Old)
1 part Premier (Bols)
1 part fresh lime juice
1 teaspoon Martini bitters (Martini)

Glass: cocktail glass

Shake the bourbon, Premier (orange curaçao), fresh lime juice and Martini bitters in a shaker. Serve in a cocktail glass.

Note: This cocktail was submitted to the second *Artist of Artists* New Cocktail Contest held by the Cocktail Communication Society in Tokyo in 1997. The theme of the contest was *cocktails for men*.

JAPANESE SEASONS

SHUNGYO 春暁

Starting in the fall of 1982, Bar l'Osier began having four cocktail fairs every year, one for every season. Until 1980, the bar had mainly sold alcohol by the bottle, which is fairly common in Japan. (A guest buys an entire bottle that is kept at the bar with the guest's name on it, and whenever the guest comes back, he or she is served from that bottle.) However, when Suntory started having its tropical cocktail competitions around 1980, the bar turned its attention to cocktails. And, as part of its efforts, it began these cocktail fairs.

Unlike cocktail competitions, fairs generally involve showcasing new cocktails, which means that you can get some pretty original creations. For me, this was a great opportunity to let my imagination run wild. Naturally, the cocktails had to be something the guests would like.

For example, three new cocktails would be unveiled each time, but

JAPANESE SEASONS

they had to differ in strength, from weak to strong, so that the guests could choose one they liked. I created Shungyo as a strong short cocktail using ingredients with a relatively high alcohol content.

The Shungyo (which means *spring dawn*) is a typical Japanese-style cocktail designed to evoke one of Japan's four seasons. In fact, it wouldn't be an exaggeration to say that it was through creating these cocktails that I succeeded in establishing my own unique style.

Cherry blossoms restored in warm water and then placed in cold water.

When creating a Japanese-style cocktail, spring is typically represented by a soft hue, summer by primary colors, fall by misty color combinations and winter by warmer colors. Japanese ingredients are used too, such as sake, shochu, umeshu (a plum liqueur) and green tea liqueurs. I decided to use sake in this cocktail.

I started by choosing a name. I wanted to evoke an image of an early spring sunrise, and to do this I planned to incorporate cherry blossoms. I used cherry blossom petals that were salted and then rinsed in warm water to dial back the saltiness. Green was the obvious choice to bring out the beauty of the flower petals. Menthe or Midori were too bright for an early spring morning, so I chose a green tea liqueur. I used vodka as a foundation to push the flavor of the Japanese sake to the fore. And, while there is indeed more vodka in the recipe, this is essentially a sake-base cocktail.

- 1 part Japanese sake (rice wine)
- 2 parts vodka (Smirnoff)
- 1 teaspoon green tea liqueur (Hermes)
- Salted cherry blossom petals

Glass: cocktail glass

Stir the sake, vodka and green tea liqueur in a mixing glass. Serve in a cocktail glass and garnish with cherry blossoms.

Note: This cocktail was created for the spring cocktail fair at Bar l'Osier in 1983.

SUMIDAGAWA BOSHOKU

Tadao Nakano, costume designer for a play called *Sumidagawa Boshoku* (*Dusk Colors on the Sumida River*), had a one-man show at Ginza Komatsu, and the opening party was held at the Shiseido Parlor where I worked at the time. There were over 100 guests, and I created this cocktail to commemorate the event.

The invitation to the party had a photograph of a kimono that was decorated with a pattern of cherry blossoms scattered on a background of the blue Sumida River. In fact, this was the kimono worn by Yukiyo Toake in the play. The image of the cocktail came to me as soon as I saw this kimono.

I wanted to modify the sake and vodka-base Shungyo by placing the cherry blossom petals inside a slightly purplish light blue. The finely hued colors meant that choosing the ingredients was going to be key in creating this cocktail.

I succeeded in achieving the purplish blue by mixing the blue of blue curaçao with the pink of a rosé vermouth, but the real key is to achieve a pale color that allows the color of the cherry blossoms to come through. To this end, you have to measure the blue curaçao very accurately. The fine color balance is lost if the proportions are not accurate. The preparation requires considerable precision.

Thanks to the rosé vermouth, this cocktail tastes a bit sweeter than the Shungyo, but the light flavor nevertheless has a full character.

The Sumidagawa Boshoku is thus a recreation of one scene of the eponymous play.

- 1 part Japanese sake
- 1 part vodka (Smirnoff)
- 1 part rosé vermouth (Martini)
- 1/2 teaspoon blue curaçao (Bols)
- Salted cherry blossom petals

Glass: cocktail glass

Stir the sake, vodka, rosé vermouth and blue curaçao in a mixing glass. Serve in a cocktail glass and garnish with the cherry blossom petals.

Note: This cocktail was created to commemorate the opening party for a one-man show of works by Tadao Nakano, an Edo Yuzen-style dyer, in July, 1995.

HIDERIBOSHI

The Hideriboshi (which is the traditional Japanese name for the star Antares) is one of a series of Japanese-style cocktails that I created using Japanese ingredients. This one uses watermelon, which is only available in Japan between June and August, and many people specifically visit my bar during this period to order this drink.

When I'm creating a Japanese-style cocktail, I first give thought to the ingredient that will be the focus of the flavor. In Japan, summer equals watermelon, and while people don't generally drink watermelon juice in Japan, I tried straining some through a cloth and found the flavor to be surprisingly strong and very impressive. One sip, and I knew instantly that umeshu would be a perfect match, so I decided to use these two very Japanese ingredients.

For the umeshu, I chose Choya Black label, which has a brandy base, because it's sweeter than Choya's other offerings, and the brandy has a full flavor. For the shochu, I used a continuous distillation type, which goes by the generic name of *white liquor*. Vodka, which is readily available in most bars, will do in a pinch.

The shochu adds the alcohol punch, the umeshu rounds out the flavor and the watermelon juice boosts the volume. What brings all these flavors together, however, is the sourness of lemon juice. By using lemons, which have a stronger sour component than limes, the sweetness of the ingredients is nicely contrasted.

Watermelon liqueur has recently become available, and it's okay to use a little bit to add some fragrance, but it has a rather artificial flavor, so be careful not to use too much.

The red color of the watermelon inspired me to name the cocktail after Antares, which shines bright red in the constellation Scorpio. Another name for Antares in Japanese is *sakeyoiboshi, the drunk star*.

1/3 shochu (continuous distilled)
1/3 umeshu (Choya Black label)
1/3 fresh watermelon juice
1 teaspoon fresh lemon juice

Glass: cocktail glass

The watermelon juice is made by chopping up watermelon flesh into small pieces and straining them through a cloth.

Shake the shochu, umeshu, fresh watermelon juice and fresh lemon juice in a shaker. Serve in a cocktail glass.

Note: This cocktail was created for the publication of my book *Cocktail Notes* (Shibata Shoten) in 1989.

SEKISHU

After Bar l'Osier underwent some renovations, the seasonal cocktail fairs were brought back as part of their marketing campaign for re-opening. The Sekishu is the cocktail I created for the full fair the year after the renovations were complete. This is another of my original cocktails on the theme of Japan's four seasons.

I didn't want to invoke the freshness of early autumn but rather deep fall bordering on winter. I wanted to use a color that would be a perfect backdrop to emphasize the bright red colors of the fallen leaves, thereby embodying the remains of fall in the green mountains.

The best backdrop to a fiery red is moss green. I set out to create a subtle hue, as I had with the combination of whiskey and blue curaçao in the King's Valley.

Whiskey is too pale to create a deep green, so I started with cognac, which has a deep flavor and amber color as a base, and added the yellow of mirabelle (a yellow plum liqueur) to achieve an expressively autumn-like color.

I chose fresh lime juice for the sour ingredient. Limes have a softer center than lemons, and therefore tend to be more refreshing. Lemons, in contrast, have a more powerful sourness. Keep these characteristics in mind when using sour ingredients in order to achieve a desired flavor most effectively.

A note about the red leaf used in the glass: I collect a lot of these bright red leaves at the end of autumn, wash them thoroughly and then dry them out, storing them like pressed flowers. In this way, I have them available in my bar year-round.

I named this cocktail last. Sekishu is a poetic word meaning *regret for the passing of autumn* and is one of the seasonal words used in haiku. I found it in a collection of seasonal words.

> 2 parts cognac (Hennessy VS)
> 1 part mirabelle (Oldesloer)
> 1 part fresh lime juice
> 1 teaspoon blue curaçao
> Autumn leaf

Glass: cocktail glass

Shake the cognac, mirabelle (yellow plum liqueur), fresh lime juice and blue curaçao in a shaker.

Note: This cocktail was created for the fall cocktail fair after Bar l'Osier was renovated.

YUKITSUBAKI

I created the Yukitsubaki in 1994 for Bar l'Osier's winter fair. This cocktail represents the bright red of a camellia flower (*tsubaki*) topped by pure white snow (*yuki*).

I had seen Yukiyo Toake in the play *Fuyu no Tsubaki* (*Winter Camellias*) and wanted to create a cocktail that would evoke the red flowers and the snow as an expression of the Japanese winter ~ a warm color combination that was still appropriate for winter.

I based the Yukitsubaki on a cocktail I created in 1974 called a Hanatsubaki. The Hanatsubaki is a shaken brandy-base cocktail that combines crème de framboise, crème de cassis and fresh lime juice. I successfully used cassis together with the still relatively unknown crème de framboise to give the drink novelty and a full flavor.

For the Yukitsubaki, I replaced the Hanatsubaki's brandy with vodka to get a clearer dark crimson color that would emphasize the whiteness of the snow.

Since this cocktail calls for a float of fresh cream, and this has a tendency to coagulate if the sourness is too strong, I toned down the sourness. If you whip the cream lightly and create a froth, the result floats beautifully on the surface of the cocktail. Using a thicker cream creates a richer flavor, which is what I recommend.

3 parts vodka (Smirnoff)
1 part crème de framboise (Gabriel)
1 part crème de cassis (Lejay)
1 part fresh cream

Glass: cocktail glass

Shake the vodka, crème de framboise and crème de cassis in a shaker. Pour into a cocktail glass and float lightly whipped fresh cream on the surface, pouring it along the barspoon.

Note: This cocktail was created for Bar l'Osier's winter cocktail fair in 1994.

CORAL FROSTED-STYLE COCKTAILS

COSMIC CORAL　　　コズミック・コーラル

This is one of the four coral frosted-style cocktails I have created. I call this the C&C series, after the initials of all the cocktails.

I had already made the City Coral when I decided I wanted to create a series. I wanted all the cocktails in the series to 1) use a variety of white spirits 2) use fresh grapefruit juice 3) use tonic water 4) have coral frosting on the outside of the glass, but change the hues of both the cock-

CORAL FROSTED-STYLE COCKTAILS

tail and the coral, and 5) christen them all with names beginning with the letter C. The second in the series became the Cosmic Coral.

This cocktail was created for the fall fair, so I wanted a name that would have something to do with the season. When you think of fall in Japan the beautiful night sky comes to mind, so I chose the name *cosmic* to evoke the dark sky splashed with twinkling stars.

My image of the autumn night sky is of a dark blue, almost a diluted blackness. I decided to use the ink blue color that I had discovered when I made the Misty in 1984. This is a deep blue created by adding a touch of grenadine to the blue curaçao made by Bols.

A red coral frosting would match this ink-like blue. My aim was to use the grenadine to create a red coral reef floating in the night sky and shining like Antares. Without the ink blue this red falls flat, so you have to make certain the blue is bright.

Tip: it's easier for the salt to attach to the grenadine if the grenadine is diluted a bit. Also, you might notice that this cocktail breaks rule No. 2 above, but the grapefruit juice was just too yellow, so I had to use fresh lime juice instead.

| 1 ounce vodka (Smirnoff)
| 2/3 ounce blue curaçao (Bols)
| 1/3 ounce fresh lime juice
| 1 teaspoon grenadine (Meijiya) + enough to create the frosting
| Tonic water

Glass: coral glass (room temperature)

Create the coral frosting on the coral glass using grenadine and salt. Shake the vodka, blue curaçao, fresh lime juice and grenadine in a shaker. Pour into the glass and fill with tonic water. Include two or three pieces of ice from the shaker. The height of the drink should match the coral line around the glass.

Note: This cocktail was created for Bar l'Osier's fall cocktail fair in 1985.

CASTARY CORAL　キャスタリー・コーラル

Cocktails have to have names that inspire dreams, and I often look to movies, plays, novels and myths for ideas. Castary is the name of a spring in Greek mythology. It actually took me quite a while to find a name that began with C and that matched the season and my image of the cocktail.

This is the third installment in my C&C series. As a base this time, I decided to use white rum with a green coral frosting.

CORAL FROSTED-STYLE COCKTAILS

Melon liqueur, crème de menthe and banana liqueur are all green. Since mint and banana have very strong flavors, I chose Midori, a melon liqueur. As you know, the coral frosting uses salt, which makes the green of the Midori pale. I fixed this by adding a bit of blue curaçao to the Midori, creating a much brighter green.

A color that would match the green of the coral is pink, and since this cocktail was made for a spring fair, I decided to go with a strawberry liqueur. This is a cocktail that has a light, airy color and is decorated with green coral frosting. The pink of pink cherry blossom petals scattered in the air reflects the green of the young leaves, creating a very spring-like image.

I initially used Bacardi white rum, but now I use Lemon Hart.

- 2/3 ounce white rum (Lemon Hart)
- 2/3 ounce crème de fraise (Pages)
- 2/3 ounce fresh grapefruit juice
- 1 teaspoon grenadine (Meijiya)
- Tonic water
- Melon liqueur plus a dash of blue curaçao for coral frosting

Glass: coral glass (room temperature)

Create the coral frosting on the glass with the melon liqueur, blue curaçao and salt. Shake the white rum, crème de fraise (strawberry liqueur), fresh grapefruit juice and grenadine in a shaker. Pour into the glass and fill with tonic water. Include two or three pieces of ice from the shaker. The height of the drink should match the coral line around the glass.

Note: This cocktail was created for Bar l'Osier's spring cocktail fair in 1986.

CRYSTAL CORAL

The C&C series originally consisted of just three cocktails, the summer City Coral, the fall Cosmic Coral and the spring Castary Coral. Only winter was missing, so naturally I had to fill that gap. I created this cocktail when our bar was featured in *Ginza Hyakuten*, a small community magazine.

Winter → snow → snowflakes → crystal is the chain of associations I followed to arrive at the concept for this drink, and I gave it the name Crystal Coral.

CORAL FROSTED-STYLE COCKTAILS

Snow is obviously white, but if you look closely at the color of a snowstorm during the day, it's actually slightly blue. I chose the last white spirit, tequila, as the base. I used just a dash of blue curaçao for the coloring and added Cointreau, which is colorless. You have to make sure that you use only a little bit of blue curaçao to create this color. The point is to create a cold color that evokes the color of crystal, therefore, do not use too much blue curaçao.

I used Cointreau for the coral frosting, and didn't add any color, leaving it white as the driven snow.

Ordinarily you chill cocktail glasses, but coral glasses are not chilled. Chilling causes condensation to form, and condensation prevents the salt from sticking properly, which ruins the coral frosting effect.

- 2/3 ounce tequila (Sauza)
- 2/3 ounce fresh grapefruit juice
- 2/3 ounce Cointreau + enough for the coral frosting
- 1/2 teaspoon blue curaçao (Bols)
- Tonic water

Glass: coral glass

Create the coral frosting on the glass with the Cointreau (white curaçao) and salt. Shake the tequila, Cointreau, fresh grapefruit juice and blue curaçao in a shaker. Pour into the glass and fill with tonic water. Include two or three pieces of ice from the shaker. The height of the drink should match the coral line around the glass.

Note: This cocktail was created for inclusion in *Ginza Hyakuten* in 1991.

CORAL 21

While not an official member of the C&C Series, this is another cocktail that uses the coral frosting.

I had always wanted to attempt a coral-style drink with a liqueur base, and that opportunity came in 1998 when C.C.S. wanted to showcase a Cointreau-base cocktail for the May issue of their magazine. Using Cointreau instead of the white spirit that was part of the C&C Series, I created a galactic color in honor of the soon-to-come 21st century.

CORAL FROSTED-STYLE COCKTAILS

As in the case of the four members of the C&C Series, I focused on choosing a color for the coral frosting that went well with the color of the cocktail. For this drink I picked Passoā, a light pink passion fruit liqueur with a strong flavor, which meant that the coral frosting would not only create a beautiful visual effect but also add to the flavor. This was another differentiating factor from the original series.

You can use fluted champagne glasses for the coral-style cocktails, but I use specially made modifications of champagne glasses for the coral drinks. These glasses are rounder at the bottom than typical fluted glasses. I use these coral glasses for all the coral cocktails. They are available for purchase at my bar, Tender.

- 1 ounce Cointreau
- 2/3 ounce fresh grapefruit juice
- 1/3 ounce blue curaçao (Bols)
- Tonic water
- Passion fruit liqueur (Passoā)

Glass: coral glass (room temperature)

Create the coral frosting on the glass with the Passoā (passion fruit liqueur) and salt. Shake the Cointreau (white curaçao), fresh grapefruit juice and blue curaçao in a shaker. Pour into the glass and fill with tonic water. Include two or three pieces of ice from the shaker. The height of the drink should match the coral line around the glass.

Note: This cocktail was created for inclusion in May issue of the *C.S.S.* magazine in 1998.

MISCELLANEOUS COCKTAILS

M-30 RAIN

Every once in a while I'll get a request to create an original cocktail for a celebrity, and the M-30 Rain cocktail was one of those. It was made for Ryuichi Sakamoto, the composer and actor who had written the score for and acted in the Academy Award–winning film *The Last Emperor*. As a theme I picked the song *Rain*, the thirtieth of the forty-four songs in the movie as well as his favorite. The M stands for *musical number*.

I started by asking what his preferences were (this is a gift, after all, so the question is important). He said he liked a light, clear flavor in a drink. I thought about it.

A cocktail called the M-45 was the basis for the M-30, and it was a drink Mr. Sakamoto liked, so I decided to make something like it.

Using the 4:1:1 ratio, I wanted to evoke the color of falling rain. Preferring something close to a light gray rather than a pretty aqua color, I decided to reproduce a color called *blue tinged gray*. To this end, I combined a pampelmuse liqueur and just a bit of blue curaçao. Pampelmuse is a liqueur with a slightly bitter, light flavor that has the ability to bring out the hidden flavors of other ingredients. This bitterness was a perfect match for the cryptic motif of the song.

You have to be careful with the amount of blue curaçao you put in. Unfortunately, if you put too much in, the color of your cocktail will go from wistful rain to the exuberant Mediterranean. Remember, you can always add more, but you can't remove it, so use only a little.

4 parts vodka (Smirnoff)
1 part pampelmuse (Specht)
1 part fresh lime juice
1/2 teaspoon blue curaçao

Glass: cocktail glass

Shake the vodka, pampelmuse (grapefruit liqueur), fresh lime juice and blue curaçao in a shaker. Serve in a cocktail glass.

Note: This cocktail was created as a gift for the composer Ryuichi Sakamoto.

BLUE TRIP

I improvised this cocktail one night when the illustrator Seiko Kawaguchi asked me to make something using tequila, her favorite liquor. She was dressed that summer night in bright cobalt blue. The color, one of my favorites, made quite a visual impact, so I made a cocktail that would match her dress. It's not uncommon to serve ladies drinks that match the color of their clothes, rings, earrings and other accessories.

Colors and names are all well and good, of course, but you can't forget the flavor. Both a cocktail's color and name are important additions that help create the overall impact. They aren't the heart of the cocktail, though.

So: cobalt blue. I knew that I could more or less create green by combining blue curaçao with fresh lime juice, but that wasn't close enough to the color she was wearing. By adding Midori as a booster, I succeeded in creating a breathtakingly vivid cobalt blue.

This is a very subtle color. Using too much or too little Midori will have a radical effect on the cocktail's impact. The recipe lists one teaspoon, but it's actually closer to half than a whole teaspoon. Be careful not to use too much.

Since it adds greater weight to the contents, a fuller, rounder glass better presents the color of this cocktail than a slim glass.

> 4 parts tequila (Sauza)
> 1 part blue curaçao (Bols)
> 1 part fresh lime juice
> 1 teaspoon melon liqueur (Midori)

Glass: cocktail glass

Shake the tequila, blue curaçao, fresh lime juice and melon liqueur in a shaker. Serve in a cocktail glass.

Note: This cocktail was improvised on the spot for the illustrator Seiko Kawaguchi.

HONG KONG
CONNECTION

This jade-hued beauty is something I created on the spot for a guest who requested something made with brandy. I combined blue curaçao with the brandy to achieve this fascinating color. And since I was improvising, the unexpectedness of the color was very effective.

MISCELLANEOUS COCKTAILS

At first, the color was a bit dull, so I added some Chartreuse, a botanical liqueur that the guest particularly liked. There is always a bit of a challenge in making new cocktails from old ingredients. The guest named the cocktail a *Hong Kong Connection* because the jade color made him think of Hong Kong.

This cocktail uses two very sweet ingredients ~ brandy and Chartreuse ~ but the fresh lime juice successfully counteracts the sweetness and prevents the flavor from becoming cloying.

When you create a cocktail as a gift for someone, you have to make it to his or her taste. That's obviously a requirement, but what this means is that it's not necessarily going to be a cocktail that everyone will like. It's a more private thing. So, if you serve it to someone else, you'll naturally want to make some modifications.

The person I made this cocktail for came in a few days later, and I wrote the recipe down on a postcard that matched the image of the cocktail and gave it to him. This was a little something that solidified the image of the cocktail for me and was fun to do. The guest also seemed to appreciate it. He told me that he had the cocktail made at another bar he frequents, but that they had trouble achieving the same color.

> 4 parts cognac (Hennessy VS)
> 1 part yellow Chartreuse
> 1 part fresh lime juice
> 1 teaspoon blue curaçao

Glass: cocktail glass

Shake the cognac, chartreuse, fresh lime juice and blue curaçao in a shaker. Serve in a cocktail glass.

Note: This cocktail was made as a special order for a particular cocktail connoisseur.

FISHERMAN
& SON

The light from the bar passes through the glass and recreates the gentle aquamarine hue of the ocean undulating beneath a bright sun.

A guest whose father had worked as the captain of a fishing boat asked me to create a cocktail that would remind him of his father. The result was the Fisherman & Son. What a great name.

The name set, I decided to create a cocktail that would evoke the sea, and went with a basic 4:1:1 short drink with rum as the base. The flavor would be similar to a Daiquiri-type cocktail.

To create the color of the ocean and to add sweetness, I chose an orange liqueur called Premier and blue curaçao. The mixing was perfect as the pale amber color of the Premier came together very well with the blue curaçao to suggest the aquamarine of the ocean.

This recipe calls for one teaspoon of blue curaçao, but you should aim for just a dash more than this. A fine balance must be struck because even just a bit more or less will prevent you from creating the right color. The important thing is to picture the color in your mind, relax and focus.

> 4 parts white rum (Bacardi)
> 1 part Premier (Bols)
> 1 part fresh lime juice
> 1 teaspoon blue curaçao

Glass: cocktail glass

Shake the white rum, Premier (orange liqueur), fresh lime juice and blue curaçao in a shaker. Serve in a cocktail glass.

Note: This cocktail was made as a gift to a guest who wanted something that would remind him of his father.

Καλος Κυμα

I love the pale yellow color of this cocktail. I used crème d'abricots (apricot brandy) in honor of Kyoko Enami's first name, which means *apricot child*. I wanted to create yellow by mixing equal amounts of crème d'abricots, which is orange, and Midori, which is green. Like the King's Valley, the Καλος Κυμα is a successful example of combining ingredients to achieve a certain color without using any ingredients of the target color (see the color combination chart). This is a cocktail that provides a fascinating visual experience.

I began with gin, which Kyoko Enami likes. I then used two different liqueurs to achieve the desired color and sweetness (since the liqueurs are not as sweet as sugar syrup, the sweetness is not cloying). In reality, this cocktail is almost like a colorful Gimlet. The addition of the gin and fresh lime juice softens the colors of the liqueurs, giving the cocktail a more feminine coloring.

Naming the cocktail required as much thought as making the drink. The Greek word for *wave* is *kyma*, which matches the last name Enami because in Japanese *nami* means *wave*. I added *kalos*, which means *beautiful*, to make *beautiful wave*. This is a wonderful match for the beautiful Kyoko Enami.

Note that the recipe calls for equal amounts of crème d'abricots and Midori, but it's better to use a little less Midori.

| 3 parts dry gin (Gordon's)
| 1 part fresh lime juice
| 1 teaspoon crème d'abricots (Lejay)
| 1 teaspoon melon liqueur (Midori)

Glass: cocktail glass

Shake the dry gin, fresh lime juice, crème d'abricots (apricot brandy) and melon liqueur in a shaker. Serve in a cocktail class.

Note: This cocktail was created as a gift for the actress Kyoko Enami on the NHK show *Fujin Hyakka* in the summer of 1992.

MIRACLE

It was a hot August day. A familiar guest sat down at the bar as always, and told me about a miracle that had happened to him that day. To commemorate the miracle, I created this cocktail, and called it a Miracle.

You can't create a cocktail as a gift for someone without knowing the person's tastes very well, and I had come up with a few new cocktails through my conversations with this guest.

He was very fond of Gimlets and wanted me to make a Gimlet variation with a slight twist.

I used dry gin as a base and added the unique yellow of mirabelle, a yellow plum liqueur that had only recently begun being imported into Japan. I liked the similarity of the words *miracle* and *mirabelle*.

I created the mood of the cocktail with one teaspoon of maraschino. Some classic cocktails use maraschino or Chartreuse to create an accent, and this is what gave me the idea.

It's important to only add a touch of maraschino, otherwise you might smother the flavor of the gin. You do want a slight aftertaste of maraschino to remain. Maraschino has a rather unique flavor, so I use a smaller amount for guests who have never had it and more for those who have.

The result: a miracle happened to the Gimlet—one teaspoon of magic.

> 4 parts dry gin (Gordon's)
> 1 part mirabelle (Oldesloer)
> 1 part fresh lime juice
> 1 teaspoon maraschino (Luxardo)

Glass: cocktail glass

Shake the dry gin, mirabelle (yellow plum liqueur), fresh lime juice and maraschino in a shaker. Serve in a cocktail glass.

Note: This is an original cocktail created for a Bar l'Osier guest in August, 1987.

MARIA ELENA

I made this cocktail for a guest who was a genuine cocktail connoisseur. In fact, a few original cocktails have been created through conversation with this guest. The Miracle, previously discussed, is one of them.

Meeting guests with whom you can engage in this kind of communication about cocktails is important. Having an acquaintance of this sort is an important asset for a bartender because the dialogue allows you to come up with cocktails that you would have never thought of on your own.

Maria Elena is a Spanish name and also a jazz standard. It also happens to be the name of a woman this particular guest met in Cuba.

Since the setting was the Caribbean, the natural base for the drink was rum. The guest could hold his liquor very well, so I used quite a large amount of rum so that the sweet aftertaste would ride on a powerful wave of alcohol.

The description of the woman he had met in Cuba inspired me to choose a soft rosé vermouth. I dialed back the sourness and added sweetness with some Cointreau in order to avoid bruising the flavor of the vermouth.

The guest really liked the drink ~ so much so that he brought a special glass to drink it out of. Since it was a private cocktail, we kept the glass in the bar just for this drink, something we normally don't do at my bar.

Tragically, this particular guest passed away very young, and together with the glass he left behind, I treasure this cocktail as an intimate reminder of him.

| 5 parts white rum (Lemon Hart)
| 1 part rosé vermouth (Martini)
| 1 teaspoon Cointreau
| 2 teaspoons fresh lime juice

Glass: cocktail glass

Mix the white rum, rosé vermouth, Cointreau (white curaçao) and fresh lime juice in a shaker. Serve in a cocktail glass.

Note: This is a private cocktail that I made for a guest in 1988 as a memento of a woman he had met in Cuba.

LAHAINA 45

The M-30 Rain is the precursor to this cocktail, which is a favorite of Kazunori Kurita, the owner of a bar called Sake Kobo Lahaina.

The Lahaina 45 was created to commemorate the ten-year anniversary of Lahaina and the 45th birthday of its owner. I made it for the party at Sake Kobo Lahaina and presented it in a little ceremony for the attendees. The name combines the name of the bar with the owner's age at the time.

Lahaina is the name of a city in Hawaii famous for whale watching. To evoke this I substituted the M-30 vodka base for rum, which is a better fit for the feel of tropical Lahaina, and chose a pampelmuse, a grapefruit liqueur that goes very well with white spirits, and fresh lime juice.

Ordinarily I add one teaspoon of a liqueur for sweetness and color to my basic 4:1:1 original cocktail ratio, and in this case I added a puolukka as an accent. Puolukka is a lingonberry liqueur that adds a soft fragrance to a cocktail.

The T-1, which is described later in this book, substitutes the blue curaçao in the M-30 with puolukka. My basic 4:1:1 format for short cocktails can be used to create many different drinks through this kind of variation.

---

4 parts white rum (Bacardi)
1 part pampelmuse (Specht)
1 part fresh lime juice
1 teaspoon puolukka (Lapponia)

Glass: cocktail glass

Mix the white rum, pampelmuse (grapefruit liqueur), fresh lime juice and puolukka (lingonberry liqueur) in a shaker. Serve in a cocktail glass.

Note: This cocktail was created in October 1996, to commemorate the tenth anniversary of the Mito bar Sake Kobo Lahaina and the owner's 45th birthday.

MOON RIVER

A guest asked me to make a cocktail that would evoke the movie *Breakfast at Tiffany's*, and the result is this cocktail, which I improvised on the spot. I called it a Moon River, after the title tune of the movie.

Two associations came to mind immediately: (1) *Breakfast at Tiffany's* → Moon River and (2) Tiffany's → New York → bourbon.

Bourbon can be shaken without producing the particular acrid taste that scotch suffers from when shaken, and since this cocktail was being made for a male guest, I chose Old Grand-Dad, which has a robust character and is strong enough to withstand the hard shake.

A moon river is a river on whose rippling surface a pathway of moonlight is reflected. With this cocktail, I created a finish that's like scooping up a handful of moonlight, and I used this to light up the fine shards of ice floating on the surface of the liquid.

Moon River has a masculine flavor, but since it also has a romantic nuance, I like to serve it in a glass with round curves.

> 4 parts bourbon (Old Grand-Dad)
> 1 part Cointreau
> 1 part fresh grapefruit juice

Glass: cocktail glass

Mix the bourbon, Cointreau (white curaçao) and fresh grapefruit juice in a shaker. Serve in a cocktail glass.

Note: This cocktail was created as a gift for a male guest in the fall of 1985.

SOUTHERN WHISPER

サザン・
ウィスパー

This is a frozen cocktail that's great for summer. It's sweet and has a pretty low alcohol content, which means it can be enjoyed like a sherbet.

Frozen cocktails using banana and melon have been popular for a while, but I decided to innovate with an expression of the season using peaches, a truly Japanese ingredient.

A velvety smooth texture is a defining feature of my frozen cocktails. To achieve this I use fruits that can be used whole and whose pulp does not easily separate from the juice, e.g., lemons, oranges or watermelons. This makes it possible to create that smooth texture.

When making frozen cocktails it's important to pay attention to the balance between the ice and the alcohol. If you get it wrong, the intended flavor will escape you. To find the right amount of ice, fill about 70% of an eight-ounce tumbler glass with ice and crush that ice in a mixer. If there is too little ice after mixing, you can add more. Use the sound of the mixer to judge when it's ready. Different machines will make different noises, but once you hear a smooth sound, the ice should be ready. A smooth finish prevents the ice and water from separating, so the cocktail can be enjoyed to the last drop without becoming watery.

I include a straw and a spoon to allow the guest the option of enjoying the cocktail as a sherbet. During fairs I serve it in a sundae glass garnished with fresh peach slices.

I chose the name by putting a spin on the Summer Whisper I made for the 1984 summer fair.

> 2/3 ounce vodka (Smirnoff)
> 1/2 white peach in syrup
> 2/3 ounce peach liqueur (Oldesloer)
> 1/3 ounce white peach syrup
> 1/3 ounce grenadine (Meijiya)
> Crushed ice

Glass: sundae glass

Blend the vodka, white peaches in syrup, peach liqueur, grenadine syrup and crushed ice until it achieves a sherbet-like consistency. Serve in a sundae glass with a straw and spoon. It is handy to mix the peaches, peach liqueur, white peach syrup and grenadine in a mixer and keep it ready for use as nectar. It keeps for three or four days in the refrigerator.

Note: This cocktail was created for the 1991 summer fair at Bar l'Osier.

M-45 SUBARU

The theme of the fall cocktail fairs is the cosmos, and the M-45 Subaru is one of the cocktails created to evoke the starry night sky. The Cosmic Coral and the Hideriboshi are other members of this group. This cocktail brings together the three basic elements ~ base, sweet component and sour component – and it would be no exaggeration to say that it is the template for all my subsequent original cocktails, including the M-30, the Lahaina 45, the T-1 and other short cocktails.

Three cocktails are always made for the fairs, each with different alcohol contents ranging from strong to weak. This cocktail was created as the strong, masculine one.

Lapponia Puolukka, which is used as the sweet ingredient, was a new liqueur in Japan at the time, and I wanted to use it for one of our fairs.

I chose vodka as a base to match the Finnish puolukka. This gives the cocktail a particularly classy finish, thereby succeeding in bringing out the unique taste of the liqueur.

For the sour ingredient I used fresh lime juice, which has a large yet unassertive and rich flavor. Using fresh lime juice seems to be a common trait among my original cocktails.

Naming the cocktail was the hardest part. Subaru is the Japanese name for the Pleiades star cluster, which is given the object number M45 in the star catalogue created by the French astronomer Charles Messier. The name was suggested by a female employee at Shiseido, and the naming coincided with the release of Shinji Tanimura's new hit song *Subaru*, which made him a star.

4 parts vodka (Smirnoff)
1 part puolukka (Lapponia)
1 part fresh lime juice

Glass: cocktail glass

Shake the vodka, puolukka (lingonberry liqueur) and fresh lime juice in a shaker. Serve in a cocktail glass.

This cocktail was made for the 1985 fall fair at Bar l'Osier.

FRAISE RICHESSE

フレイズ・リシェス

Fraise Richesse means something like *the luxuriousness of strawberries* in French. At a time when champagne was undergoing an unprecedented boom, this cocktail combined fresh strawberries, a symbol of spring, with the tangy taste of champagne. This is a luxurious cocktail if ever there was one.

The subtle bouquet and flavor of the champagne, which is the selling point of this cocktail, should be brought together as naturally as possible with the color and flavor of the strawberries. Be careful not to add

MISCELLANEOUS COCKTAILS

too much grenadine. Since the role of the grenadine is just to support the sweetness of the crème de fraise and to fill out the red hue of the strawberry juice, it needs to be added in just the right amount.

When blending the ingredients, try to leave some of the flesh of the strawberries intact to add a bit of their texture in the drink.

I don't think there's any real need to specify the brand of champagne or the type of strawberries. Those flavors are not really the focus. It is the original intent of the cocktail that is important. Accordingly, any type of brut (dry) champagne will do.

The strawberries, too, just need to be fresh and in-season. The type or size doesn't matter. Keep in mind that you'll be mixing them with brut champagne, so a sweeter type is better.

I served this drink in a fluted champagne glass for the fair, but other options are a large wine glass or a small goblet.

2/3 ounce crème de fraise (Pages)
3 strawberries
2 teaspoons grenadine (Meijiya)
Brut champagne

Glass: *wine glass*

Blend the crème de fraise (strawberry liqueur), strawberries and grenadine in a mixer and pour into a wine glass or fluted champagne glass. Fill with chilled champagne. At the fair I used a nectar of blended fresh strawberries and grenadine. Remember to leave some of the texture of the strawberries. The cocktail should be consumed that day, as the flavor and color will turn.

Note: This cocktail was made for the 1984 spring fair at Bar l'Osier.

BRUME D'OR

ブリューム・ドール

I created the Brume d'Or for a guest who was celebrating his birthday.

Being a celebration, I used champagne and mixed in some gold leaf flakes, creating a cocktail with a decidedly festive mood.

The secret of this cocktail lies in how well you can present the gold leaf flakes using the carbonation in the champagne. Giving the cocktail

MISCELLANEOUS COCKTAILS

a color that best shows off the gold is important. I chose to create a pale blue-green using blue curaçao and grapefruit juice.

Brume means *fog* or *mist* in French, and *or* means *gold*, so the name can be translated as *Gold Mist*. A hard shake breaks up the gold leaf flakes into very small pieces, which will then float up on the bubbles in the champagne. The champagne is poured in after the gold flakes, creating a crown-like effect at the surface of the fluted champagne glass. If the carbonation in the champagne is still strong, the surface of the drink actually puffs up a bit, creating a nice effect. For that effect I recommend using just opened champagne.

This drink falls in the category of apéritifs made with champagne and fresh fruit juice, and the flavor is based on the Angel cocktail that I made in 1988 ($1/3$ ounce Cointreau, 1 ounce fresh grapefruit juice, 1 teaspoon grenadine syrup and champagne). For the Brume d'Or, I replaced the grenadine with blue curaçao. The alcohol content is low and the flavor is very accessible, so I often make it for guests who are celebrating their birthdays.

$1/3$ ounce Cointreau
1 ounce fresh grapefruit juice
1 teaspoon blue curaçao (Bols)
Edible gold leaf flakes
Brut champagne

Glass: fluted champagne glass

Shake the Cointreau (white curaçao), fresh grapefruit juice, blue curaçao and gold leaf flakes in a shaker. Pour into a fluted champagne glass and fill with champagne.

Note: This cocktail was created in 1989 as a present for a guest who was celebrating his birthday.

TENDER SERIES

All of the original cocktails that I've described so far have been created for either contests or as gifts, but now I'm going to talk about a couple of cocktails I created specifically for my own bar, Tender.

I decided to take the first letter of Tender and add a number to it for each cocktail, the number increasing as I create a new commemorative cocktail annually.

I had a strong feeling that I could expand this into a series when I created the T-1. I'm thinking of putting together a large collection of my own original cocktails based on my basic short drink format of 4:1:1.

Fixed rules and the potential for broad variations would be essential for the series to grow. Therefore, I decided that the T Series would be defined by three basic characteristics: 1) all the drinks would have a white spirit base, since white spirits allow for the most modifications in color and flavor 2) they would all use fresh lime juice for its soft sour flavor and 3) they would all have subtle colorings, the hallmark of my cocktails.

The basic pattern for the cocktails in the T Series is base liquor + additional ingredients (a liqueur for sweetness and a liqueur for color) + fresh lime juice. As long as I can shake that shaker, I intend to create a new one each year, watching the number grow.

The cocktail I made for the first anniversary of Tender was the T-1. The Lahaina 45 was its precursor, the T-1 using vodka instead of the Lahaina 45's white rum. The Lahaina 45 was itself a modification of the M-30 Rain, however, substituting the vodka with white rum and the blue curaçao with puolukka. So you could say that the T-1 is a thoroughbred born from a pairing of the M-30 Rain and the Lahaina 45.

It is a cocktail that has a soft pink shade thanks to the fine bubbles created by the hard shake.

I used gin as the white spirit in the T-2, which was created for the second anniversary. Gin has a unique flavor that calls attention to itself, so I actually had quite a bit of trouble pairing a liqueur with it.

T-1

T-2

TENDER SERIES

Flavored liqueurs like puolukka and pampelmuse don't work well with gin, so I selected Cointreau and mirabelle, both flavors that wouldn't clash with the base, creating a pale yellow cocktail. It could be called a modification of the White Lady, substituting the lemon juice with fresh lime juice.

T-1 Tender One

4 parts vodka (Smirnoff)
1 part pampelmuse (Specht)
1 part fresh lime juice
1 teaspoon puolukka (Lapponia)

Glass: cocktail glass

Shake the vodka, pampelmuse (grapefruit liqueur), fresh lime juice and puolukka (lingonberry liqueur) in a shaker. Serve in a cocktail glass.

Note: This cocktail was created in the summer of 1998 to commemorate the first anniversary of the opening of Tender.

T-2 Tender Two

4 parts dry gin (Gordon's)
1 part Cointreau
1 part fresh lime juice
1 teaspoon mirabelle (Oldesloer)

Glass: cocktail glass

Shake the dry gin, Cointreau (white curaçao), fresh lime juice, and Mirabelle (yellow plum liqueur) in a shaker. Serve in a cocktail glass.

Note: This cocktail was created in the summer of 1999 to commemorate the second anniversary of the opening of Tender.

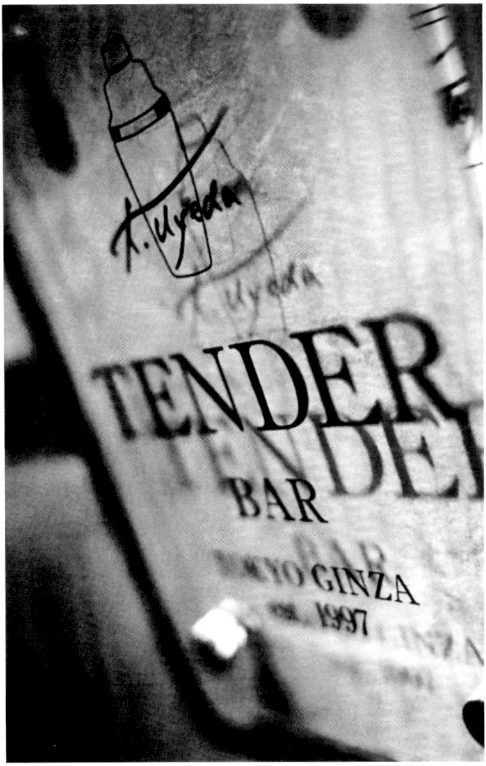
TENDER
BAR
GINZA
1997

INDEX

A
Apple brandy, 62
Awareness, focusing, 16–17

B
Barspoons
- choosing, 69
- holding, 36
- pouring drink down, 39
- for stirring, 34, 36–37
- types of, 69
- using, 36–37

Basic techniques, 43–56
- coral frosting, 54–55
- cracking ice, 47–50
- cutting fruit, 55–56
- holding bottle, 44–45
- holding glass, 51
- layering, 52–53
- measuring ingredients, 43–44, 46–47
- peeling lemons, 50–51
- polishing glasses, 52
- refining drinking experience of guests, 43
- removing cap, 45
- rim frosting, 53–54
- using jiggers, 43, 47

Bottle
- holding, 44–45
- removing cap, 45

Bourbon, 61, 63
Brandies, 60, 62
Brown spirits, 60–63
- about: overview of, 60
- dark rum, 62
- defined, 60
- types of whiskey, 60. *See also* Whiskey
- whiskey compatibilities in cocktails, 63

Building techniques, 38–42
- with carbonated drinks, 38, 40–41
- with non-carbonated drinks, 38, 41–42
- pousse-café style, 39, 42
- types of, 38–39

C
Canadian whiskey, 60, 63
Cap, removing, 45
Carbonated drinks, building, 38, 40–41
Color(s)
- combinations of, 136
- how they add to flavor, 135–136
- wheel, cocktail examples on, 137

Coral frosting, 54–55
Customers. *See* Guests

D
Dark rum, 62

F
Focus(ing)
- on all six senses, 19
- boosting, 16–17
- on both results and process, 19–20
- on every movement, 43
- importance of, 16–17
- on shaking process, 23
- on stirring, 32

of Westerners compared to Japanese, 19–20
Frosting glasses
　coral frosting, 54–55
　rim frosting, 53–54
Fruit
　cutting, 55–56
　peeling lemons, 50–51

G

Gin, 57–58
Glasses
　coral frosting, 54–55
　frosting rims, 53–54
　holding, 51
　importance of, 70
　matching cocktails to, 70
　polishing, 52
　rocks, 71
　rounded, 71
　thickness of, 70
　triangular, 71
　tumblers, 71
　types of, 71
　wine, 71
Grape brandy, 62
Guests
　fine-tuning cocktails to their liking, 20
　how you present yourself to, 20
　importance of their opinion, 20
　knowing preferences of, 17–18, 20–21
　making cocktails they love, 21
　techniques to refine drinking experience of. *See* Basic techniques

H

Holding
　barspoons, 36
　bottle, 44–45
　glasses, 51
　mixing glass, 37
　shakers, 28

I

Ice
　cracking techniques, 47–50
　finding grain of, 47
　fine shards of, hard shake and, 26
　making cracked ice, 48
　making spheres, 49–50
　stirring and, 31, 32, 33, 35
　temperature chart, 33
Imai, Kiyoshi, 17–18

J

Japanese approach to making cocktails, 18–21
Japanese liqueurs, 65
Japanese whiskey, 60, 63
Jiggers, 43, 47, 69

L

Language of cocktails, 15
Layering cocktails, 52–53
Lemons, peeling, 50–51
Liqueurs, 64–66
　about: overview of, 64
　characteristics of, 65
　defined, 64–65
　flavoring types, 65
　how they're made, 64–65
　Japanese, 65
　selecting, 65–66

M

Making cocktails
  avoiding arrogance in, 20
  focusing while. *See* Focus(ing)
  Japanese approach to, 18-21
  knowing guests' preferences, 17-18
  language of cocktails and, 15
  making them your own, 15
  most important job in, 21
  perception of flavor and, 19-20, 21
  reading taste buds and, 17-18
  staying aware of who's drinking what, 17
  using recipes, 15
  way of the cocktail and, 18-21
  your appearance, presentation and, 20
Measuring ingredients, 43-44, 46-47
Mental focus, 16-17
Mixing glasses
  choosing, 68-69
  holding, 37
  shakers vs., 67
  types of, 69
Mr. Martini, 17-18

N

Non-carbonated drinks, building, 38, 41-42

O

Original Cocktails
  fundamental requirement of, 18
  how colors add to flavor, 135-136

P

Peeling lemons, 50-51
Perception of flavor, 19-20, 21
Polishing glasses, 52
Pouring cocktails
  after shaking, 27, 30
  down barspoon, 39
  layering technique, 52-53
Pousse-café style, 39, 42
Preferences of guest, knowing, 17-18, 20-21

R

Reading taste buds, 17-18
Recipes. *See also Drink Index*
  creating something unique from, 15
  four for every drink, 18
  modified to match current tastes, 18
  personal, 15, 18
  standard, 18
  that guests like, 18
  using, 15
Rim frosting, 53-54
Rocks glasses, 71
Rounded cocktail glasses, 71
Rum, 58-59, 62

S

Scotch whiskey, 60-61, 63
Shaken cocktails, categories of, 134
Shakers
  choosing, 67-68
  holding, 28
  mixing glasses vs., 67

with or without internal strainers, 69
types of, 23, 67, 69
uses of, 67
Shaking technique (hard shake), 22–30
    adapting based on ingredients, 24
    affecting taste of cocktails, 22–23
    fine shards of ice and, 26
    focusing energy, 23
    holding shaker, 28
    ingredients not suited for, 25
    ingredients suited for, 24–25, 57–59
    motion and angle of, 23–24, 29–30
    overview, 22, 26–27
    perfecting, 24
    pouring cocktail, 27, 30
    stance, 29–30
    step by step, illustrated, 26–30
    technique delineated, 26–30
Spheres of ice, 49–50
Spirits. *See* Brown spirits; White spirits
Stance, for hard shake, 29–30
Stirring technique, 31–37
    amounts of ice and, 35
    focusing mind on, 32
    holding and using barspoon, 36–37
    holding mixing glass, 37
    ice and, 31, 32, 33, 35
    ideal stir, 31–32
    objective of, 32
    overview, 31, 34–35
    step by step, illustrated, 34–37
    temperature chart, 33
    tools needed, 32

T

Temperature chart, 33
Tequila, 59
Tools. *See* Barspoons; Jiggers; Mixing glasses; Shakers
Triangular cocktail glasses, 71
Tumblers, 71

V

Vodka, 58

W

Way of the cocktail, 18–21
Whiskey
    Bourbon, 61
    Canadian, 60, 63
    compatibilities in cocktails, 63
    Japanese, 60, 63
    Scotch, 60–61, 63
    types of, 60
White spirits, 57–59
    about: overview of, 57
    defined, 57
    gin, 57–58
    rum, 58–59
    suited to hard shake, 57–59
    tequila, 59
    vodka, 58
Wine glasses, 71

INDEX OF DRINKS

A
Alaska, 80-81
Alexander, 94-95

B
Bacardi, 116-117
Bamboo, 130-131
Bellini, 128-129
Blue Trip, 174-175
Brandy Sour, 98-99
Brume d'Or, 196-197

C
Castary Coral, 166-167
Charlie Chaplin, 126-127
City Coral, 146-147
Coral 21, 170-171
Cosmic Coral, 164-165
Crystal Coral, 168-169

D
Daiquiri, 114-115

F
Fantastic Léman, 142-143
Fisherman & Son, 178-179
Fraise Richesse, 194-195
Frozen Daiquiri, 118-119

G
Gibson, 76-77
Gimlet, 78-79
Gimlet Highball, 88-89
Gin & Bitters, 82-83
Gin & Tonic, 84-85
Grasshopper, 122-123

H
Hideriboshi, 158-159
Hong Kong Connection, 176-177

J
Jack Rose, 96-97
Jealousy, 150-151

K
$K\alpha\lambda o\varsigma\ K\upsilon\mu\alpha$, 180-181
King's Valley, 148-149
Kir Royal, 132-133

L
Lahaina, 186-187
Left Alone, 152-153

M
M-30 Rain, 172-173
M-45 Subaru, 192-193
Manhattan, 100-101
Margarita, 120-121
Maria Elena, 184-185
Martini, 73-75
Miracle, 182-183
Moon River, 188-189
Moscow Mule, 110-111

N
New York, 102-103

O
Old Fashioned, 104-105

P
Prize-winning cocktails, 138-153
Pure Love, 138-141

R
Russian, 106-107

S
Salty Dog, 108-109
Sea Breeze, 112-113
Sekishu, 160-161

Shungyo, 154–155
Sidecar, 90–91
Southern Whisper, 190–191
Stinger, 92–93
Sumidagawa Boshoku, 156–157

T

Tender Series (T-1 and T-2), 198–201
Tokio, 144–145

V

Valencia, 124–125

W

White Lady, 86–87

Y

Yukitsubaki, 162–163

ABOUT THE AUTHOR

KAZUO UYEDA was born in August 1944, in Chanai, Hokkaido. His first bartending job was at Tokyo Kaikan in 1966. In 1974 he moved to Shiseido Parlor, where he worked as manager and chief bartender at Bar l'Osier. He participated in many competitions throughout Japan as well as in two international competitions where he represented Japan, winning many awards and gaining broad renown. He was appointed chief bartender and director of Shiseido Parlor Co., Ltd. in 1995 and proceeded to make Bar l'Osier into a bar of unshakeable reputation.

In 1994, he acted as a committee member (officer) of the Cocktail Communication Society, whose goal is to deepen communication between bartenders and guests, create a more multifarious drinking culture and raise the position of bartenders in society.

In 1997 he left Shiseido Parlor after many years of service and opened Tender in Ginza, Tokyo. Today he can be found at the bar, shaking the shaker and mixing drinks as owner and bartender. He's active in bartender education and holds many seminars throughout Japan.

His other books include *The Cocktail Book* (Seitosha), *Kazuo Uyeda's Cocktail Notes* (Shibata Shoten) and *Cocktails* (Seitosha).